ORIGAMI on the FLIP SIDE

EDITED BY CHRISTINE BYRNES

Main Street
A division of Sterling Publishing Co., Inc.
New York

Published by Sterling Publishing Co., Inc.
387 Park Avenue South, New York, NY 10016

© 2005 by Sterling Publishing Co., Inc.

This book is composed of material from the following Sterling titles:
Super Simple Origami by Irmgard Kneissler © 1996 by Urania-Ravensburger in der Dornier Medienholding GmbH
Easy Origami Animals by Ruth Ungert © 2001 by English Publication GmbH, Wiesbaden
English translation © 2003 by Sterling Publishing Co., Inc.
Origami for the First Time ® ©2003 by Soonboke Smith
Origami Holidays © 2002 by Duy Nguyen
Fantasy Origami © 2001 by Duy Nguyen
Jungle Animal Origami © 2003 by Duy Nguyen
Creepy Crawly Animal Origami © 2003 by Duy Nguyen
Under the Sea Origami © 2004 by Duy Nguyen
Dinosaur Origami © 2002 by Duy Nguyen
Amazing Origami by Kunihiko Kasahara © 2000 by Augustus Verlag in der Weltbild Ratgeber Verlage GmbH & Co. KG
English translation © 2001 by Sterling Publishing Co., Inc.
Extreme Origami by Kunihiko Kasahara © 2001 by Augustus Verlag in der Weltbild Ratgeber Verlage GmbH & Co. KG
English translation © 2002 by Sterling Publishing Co., Inc.

Origami Paper Designs:
Papers by Kate's Paperie, 212-941-9816, www.katespaperie.com

Printed in China
Sterling ISBN-13: 978-1-4027-2906-5
ISBN-10: 1-4027-2906-5

For information about custom editions, special sales, premium and
corporate purchases, please contact Sterling Special Sales
Department at 800-805-5489 or specialsales@sterlingpub.com.

2 4 6 8 10 9 7 5 3

CONTENTS

INTRODUCTION 4

BASIC INSTRUCTIONS 5

BASIC FOLDS 6

BASIC FORMS 12

   BASIC FORM II 12

   BASIC FORM III 12

   BASIC FORM IV 13

   BASIC FORM V 15

   BASIC FORM VI 16

   BASIC FORM VII 17

BASIC FORM VIII 18

PROJECTS 19

   SUPER SIMPLE ORIGAMI 21

   FLOWER FUN 43

   FARM ANIMALS 71

   WILD CREATURES 95

   AQUARIUM FUN 191

   FANTASTIC CREATURES 217

   THIS AND THAT 251

   EXTREME ORIGAMI 291

INTRODUCTION

"Origami," the simple art of paper folding, originated in Japan and was passed down by generations of Japanese who taught their children the basics, and the joy, of creating fantasy worlds from paper. With several or more folds, simple square pieces of paper become beautiful objects: animals, flowers, or even people.

Seeing these transformations, it is easy for new origami hobbyists to gain an enthusiasm that leads them to quickly improve their creative ability and artistic skills.

Selected for this book are a number of interesting figures you can create using these simple folding techniques. Each one includes step-by-step diagrams with short, clear directions that will make origami technique easy to understand and learn. The best part about *Origami on the Flip Side* is that the paper can be removed from the book to use for the project! Simply remove the sheet of paper that precedes the project, and fold away. In order to get to do all the projects, it works best if you start from the beginning and fold your way to the end. Be sure to leave the Basic Folds and Basic Form pages in the book. You'll need to reference them for the projects. The projects also start off easier, and are harder towards the end. Or, if you want to preserve the projects for future use, you can buy origami paper and keep the book intact.

Happy Folding.

BASIC INSTRUCTIONS

PAPER

The best paper to use for origami will be very thin, keep a crease well, and fold flat. It can be plain white paper, solid-color paper, or wrapping paper with a design only on one side. Regular typing paper may be too heavy to allow the many tight folds needed for some figures. Be aware, too, that some kinds of paper may stretch slightly, either in length or in width, and this may cause a problem in paper folding. Packets of paper especially for use in origami are available from craft and hobby shops.

Unless otherwise indicated, the usual paper used in creating these forms is square, 15 by 15 centimeters or approximately 6 by 6 inches. Some forms may call for half a square, i.e., 3 by 6 inches or, cut diagonally, a triangle. For those who are learning and have a problem getting their fingers to work tight folds, larger sizes of paper can be used. Actually, any size paper squares can be used—slightly larger figures are easier to make than overly small ones. The paper provided within this book is 7 $\frac{1}{2}$ by 7 $\frac{1}{2}$ inches, easy to work with for origami novices.

GLUE

Use a good, easy-flowing but not loose paper glue, but use it sparingly. You don't want to soak the paper. A toothpick makes a good applicator. Allow the glued form time to dry. Avoid using stick glue, as the application pressure needed (especially if the stick has become dry) can damage your figure.

TECHNIQUE

Fold with care. Position the paper, especially at corners, precisely, and see that edges line up before creasing a fold. Once you are sure of the fold, use a fingernail to make a clean, flat crease. Don't get discouraged with your first efforts. In time, what your mind can conceive, your fingers will fashion.

SYMBOLS & LINES

- - - - - - - - - -	- · - · - · - · - · -	◄————►	+++++++++++++++
Fold line: valley	Fold line: mountain	Fold then unfold	Cut line

⌒○➤	——➤	————
Turn over or rotate	Pleat fold (repeated folding)	Crease line

BASIC FOLDS

KITE FOLD

1 Fold and unfold a square diagonally, making a center crease.

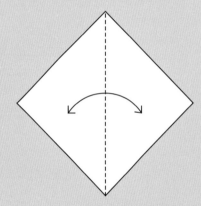

2 Fold both sides into the center crease.

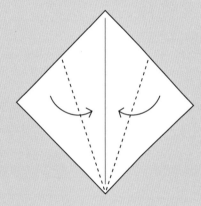

3 This is a kite form, and Basic Form I.

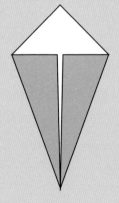

VALLEY FOLD

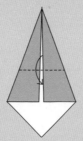

1 Here, using the kite, fold form toward you (forward), making a "valley."

2 This fold forward is a valley fold.

MOUNTAIN FOLD

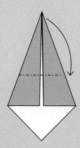

1 Here, using the kite, fold form away from you (backwards), making a "mountain."

2 This fold backwards is a mountain fold.

SINK FOLD

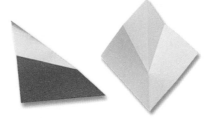

1 With the paper folded diagonally, prefold a corner diagonally downward. Undo the corner fold again.

2 Allow the figure to open slightly. On the outer side, there is to the right of the center crease a mountain fold and to the left of that crease a valley fold. Push the diagonal crease at the top of the form inward from top to the side creases, and at the same time fold the figure together diagonally again. Press the fold flat firmly from the outside.

3 The valley fold has turned into a mountain fold; and you've made a sink fold.

INSIDE REVERSE FOLD

1 Starting here with a kite, valley fold kite closed.

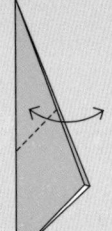

2 Valley fold as marked to crease, then unfold.

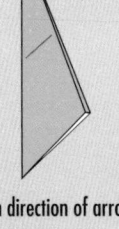

3 Pull tip in direction of arrow.

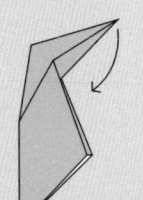

4 Appearance before completion.

5 You've made an inside reverse fold.

OUTSIDE REVERSE FOLD

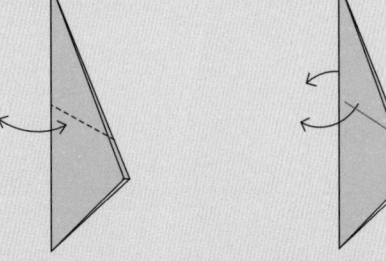

1 Using closed kite, valley fold, unfold.

2 Fold inside out, as shown by arrows.

3 Appearance before completion.

4 You've made an outside reverse fold.

PLEAT FOLD

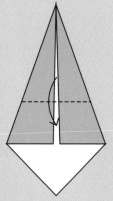

1 Here, using the kite, valley fold.

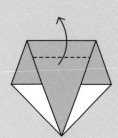

2 Valley fold back again.

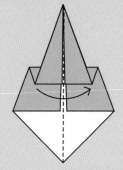

3 This is a pleat. Valley fold in half.

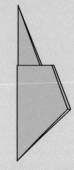

4 You've made a pleat fold.

PLEAT FOLD REVERSE

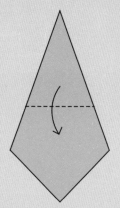

1 Here, using the kite form backwards, valley fold.

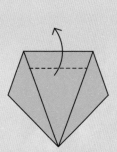

2 Valley fold back again for pleat.

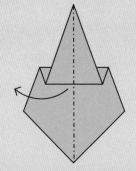

3 Mountain fold form in half.

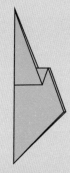

4 This is a pleat fold reverse.

SQUASH FOLD I

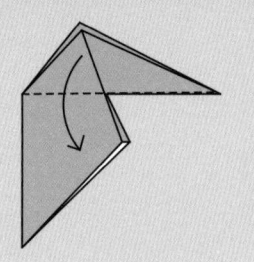

1 Using inside reverse, valley fold one side.

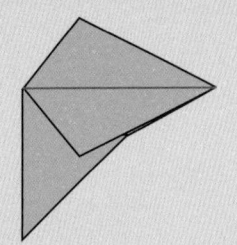

2 This is a squash fold I.

SQUASH FOLD II

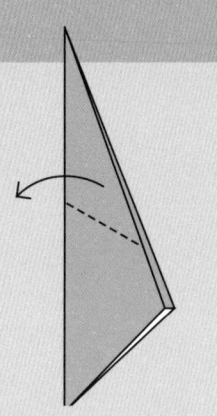

1 Using closed kite form, valley fold.

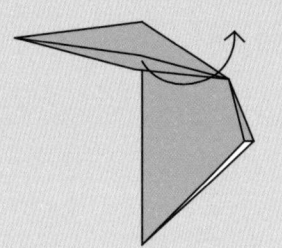

2 Open in direction of the arrow.

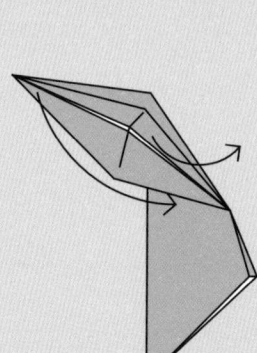

3 Appearance before completion.

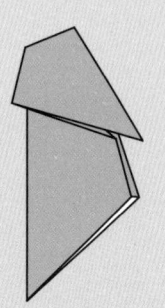

4 You've made a squash fold II.

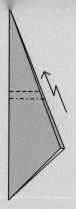

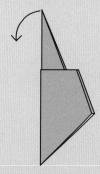

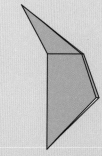

1 Here using closed kite form, pleat fold.

2 Pull tip in direction of the arrow.

3 This is an inside crimp fold.

INSIDE CRIMP FOLD

OUTSIDE CRIMP FOLD

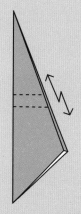

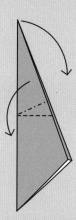

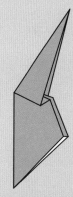

1 Here using closed kite form, pleat fold and unfold.

2 Fold mountain and valley as shown, both sides.

3 This is an outside crimp fold.

BASIC FORMS

The following basic, or base, forms are the foundations for creating the origami projects in this book. Once you have mastered these forms, you will be able to use them as a starting point and add onto them with specific folds to create a particular figure. Basic Form I is the Kite Fold, found in the Basic Folds section on page 8.

BASIC FORM II

1 Begin with a square.

2 Fold and unfold in half diagonally in both directions (wrong side of paper is on the inside).

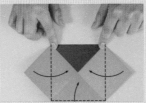

3 Fold left and right corners up along midline to meet at top corner.

4 (Completed Basic Form II.)

BASIC FORM III

1 Begin with a square. Fold in half (wrong side of paper is inside.)

2 Unfold. Rotate and fold in half in other direction.

3 Unfold to show creases. Turn model over. Fold all corners to the center.

4 (Completed Basic Form III.)

BASIC FORM IV

1 Begin with a square. Fold in half (right side of paper is inside).

2 Unfold. Rotate and fold in half in other direction (right side of paper is inside).

3 Unfold. Fold in half diagonally (wrong side of paper is inside).

4 Unfold. Rotate and fold in half diagonally in other direction (wrong side of paper is inside).

(CONTINUES)

5 Unfold. Fold bottom of edge to horizontal midline (wrong side of paper is inside).

6 Fold top edge to horizontal midline (wrong side of paper is inside).

7 Rotate and fold bottom edge to horizontal midline.

8 Fold top edge to horizontal midline.

9 Unfold last two folds. Fold the left corner up and to the right.

10 Unfold. Fold the right corner up and to the left.

11 Lift the bottom edge. Pull each corner up and pinch out.

12 Flatten this edge toward the center.

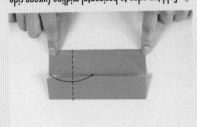

13 Repeat Steps 11–12 to fold the top edge. (Completed Basic Form IV.)

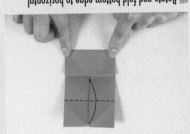

BASIC FORM V

1 Begin with a square. Fold and unfold in half diagonally in both directions (wrong side of paper is inside).

2 Rotate and fold in half (right side of paper is inside).

3 Unfold. Rotate and fold in half in other direction (right side of paper is inside).

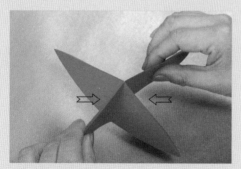

4 Unfold. Turn model over. Collapse two opposite sides to the center along the horizontal fold.

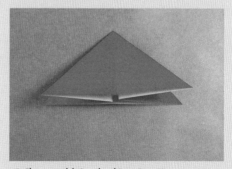

5 Flatten model. Completed Basic Form V.

BASIC FORM VI

1 Begin with a square. Fold in half (wrong side of paper is inside).

2 Unfold. Rotate and fold in half in other direction.

3 Unfold. Turn model over. Fold in half diagonally (right side of paper is inside).

4 Unfold. Fold in half diagonally in other direction (right side of paper is inside).

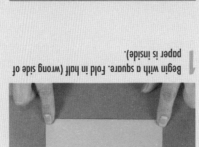

5 Unfold. Turn model over.

6 Fold two opposite side corners to meet at center.

7 Flatten model. Completed Basic Form VI.

BASIC FORM VII

1 Begin with the Basic Form VI.

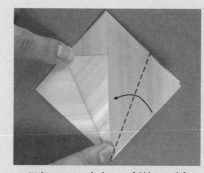

2 With opening at the bottom, fold bottom left side of upper flap to vertical midline.

3 Fold bottom right side of upper flap to vertical midline.

4 Rotate and fold folded corner of Basic Form VI up to the center.

5 Unfold last three folds.

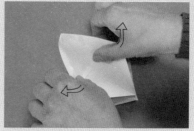

6 Rotate model and begin to form the upper wing by opening the upper flap at the bottom point, pulling it up as far as possible.

7 Press at left and right flap corners so the edges meet at the midline.

8 This will form a diamond. Turn the model over. Repeat Steps 2–7.

9 Completed Basic Form VII.

BASIC FORM VIII

1 Begin with the Kite Fold.

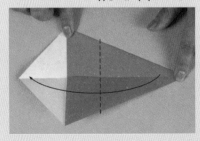

2 Rotate model and fold in half, bringing bottom corner to meet top corner.

3 Unfold last fold. Rotate model and fold bottom left side to horizontal midline.

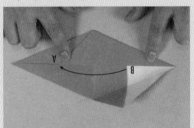

4 Rotate model and fold bottom right side to horizontal midline.

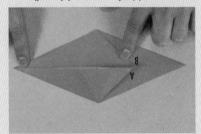

5 Unfold the last two folds.

6 Lift corner A and then pull it downward so the side point moves toward the horizontal midline.

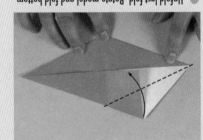

7 Rotate model. Lift corner B and then pull it downward so the side point moves toward the horizontal midline.

8 Completed Basic Form VIII.

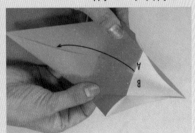

Projects

STAR

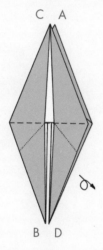

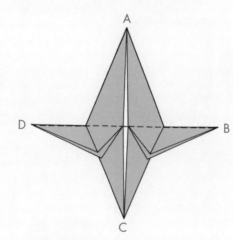

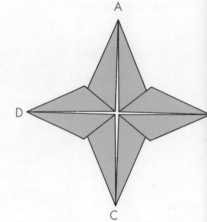

1 Start with Basic Form VII, then reverse folds to the inside at points B and D. By a valley fold in the dashed line, bring point C down, and turn the fold over.

2 Valley folds in the dashed lines at corners B and D.

3 Completed Star.

PINWHEEL

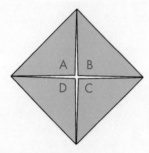

1 Start with Basic Form III. Fold corners A and C backward onto the center point.

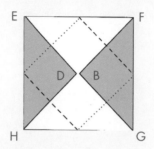

2 Fold corners F and H to the front, and corners E and G to the back, onto the center point.

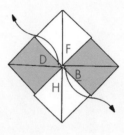

3 Pull out corners D and B, as indicated by arrows.

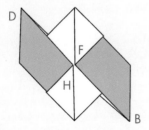

4 Completed Step 3.

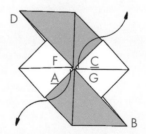

5 Pull out corners A and C in the same way.

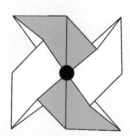

6 Completed Pinwheel.

FISH AS WIND SOCK

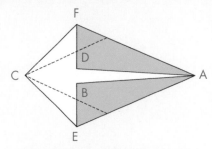

1 Start with Basic Form I, the Kite Fold. At corner C, valley fold in the dashed lines.

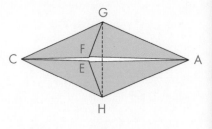

2 Valley fold in the dashed line, point C on point A.

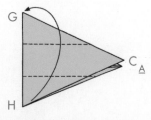

3 Valley fold in the dashed lines, then tuck corner H into corner G.

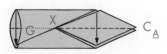

4 Form a tube from the figure obtained, and turn it into position as shown before step 5.

5 Reverse fold inside and outside at point A/C (fold together).

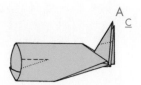

6 Reverse fold inside at point A/C. Form the mouth at the round opening by mountain and valley folds in the front and back.

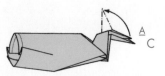

7 Fold point A upward to the fin. Fasten the mouth creases by tucking in the inside corners.

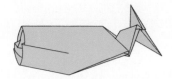

8 Completed Fish as Wind Sock.

MASK I

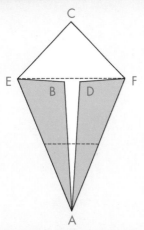

1 Start with Basic Form I, Kite Fold. Valley fold at corner C. Valley fold at point A.

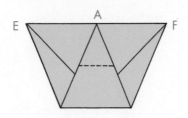

2 At point A, valley fold.

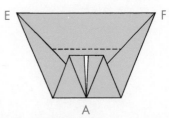

3 At corner C, valley fold.

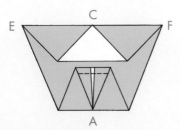

4 At point A, valley fold.

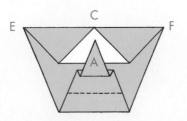

5 Valley fold at point A.

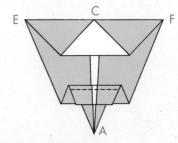

6 Valley fold at point A.

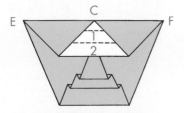

7 At corner C, valley fold in the dashed lines 1 and 2. Tuck corner C under the edge of the fold, as shown before step 8.

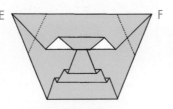

8 Mountain fold at points E and F.

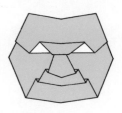

9 Completed Mask I.

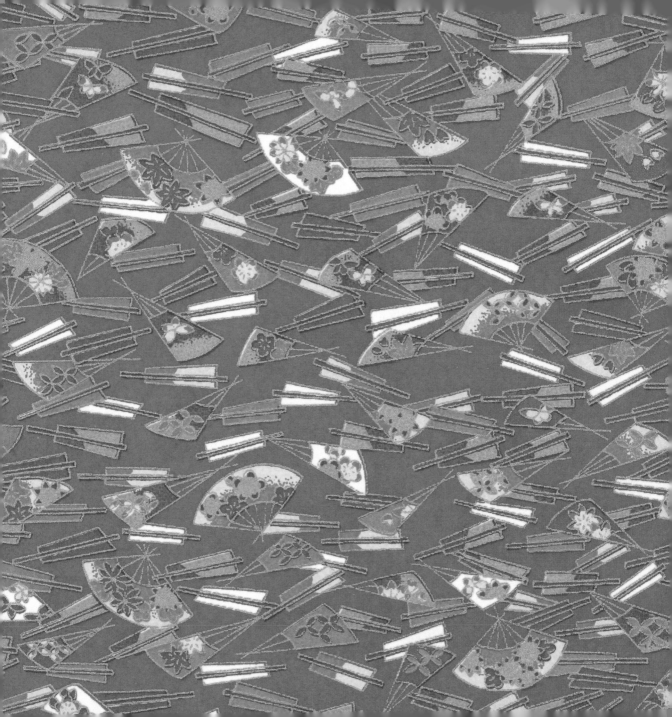

MASK II

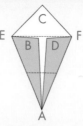

1 Start with Basic Form I, Kite Fold. Valley fold at corner C. Valley fold at point A.

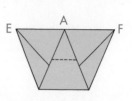

2 At point A, valley fold.

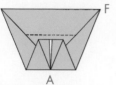

3 At corner C, valley fold.

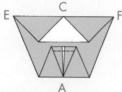

4 At point A, valley fold.

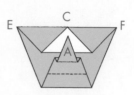

5 Valley fold at point A.

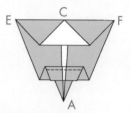

6 Valley fold at point A.

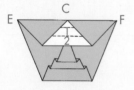

7 At corner C, valley fold in the dashed lines 1 and 2. Tuck corner C under the edge of the fold, as shown before step 8.

8 At point A, mountain fold in the dotted lines.

9 Valley fold at corners E and F.

10 Turn the fold over.

11 Valley fold at corners G and H. At points E and F, valley fold in the dashed lines, and mountain fold in the dotted lines. By doing so, points X fall into the position as shown before step 12.

12 Turn the fold over.

13 Completed Mask II.

DUCK

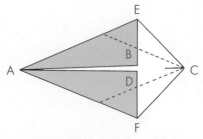

1 Start with Basic Form I, the Kite Fold. Valley fold in dashed lines.

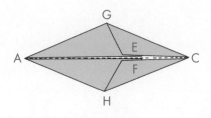

2 Valley fold in center crease.

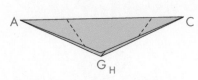

3 Reverse fold outside in the dashed lines at A and C.

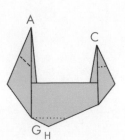

4 Reverse fold outside in the dashed line at point A. Reverse fold inside in the dotted line at point C. Mountain fold front and back at corners G and H.

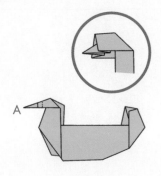

5 Reverse fold inside and outside at point A to form the beak.

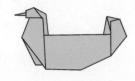

6 Completed Duck.

MONKEY

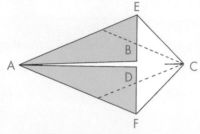

1 Start with Basic Form I, the Kite Fold. At point C, valley fold in the dashed lines.

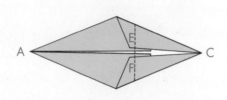

2 At point C, valley fold left into the dashed line.

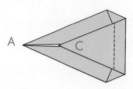

3 At point C, valley fold to the right in the dashed line.

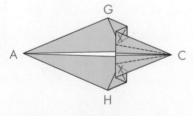

4 At point C, move the points X into the position shown in the next illustration by means of valley folds in the dashed lines and mountain folds in the dotted lines.

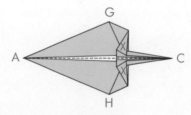

5 Valley fold in the center crease.

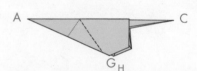

6 Valley fold in the dashed line—only the front sheet of paper. Simultaneously, pull point A into the position shown in the illustration in step 7. Crease the mountain fold that is forming in the dotted line.

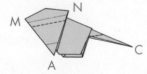

7 Form the head by means of mountain and valley folds at point A. At point C, reverse fold to the outside.

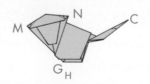

8 Form the ears at corners M and N by reverse folds inside and outside. At point C, reverse fold outside.

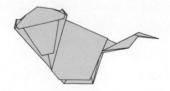

9 Completed Monkey, enlarged.

PENGUIN

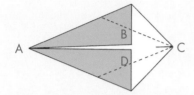

1 Start with Basic Form I, the Kite Fold. Valley fold in the dashed lines.

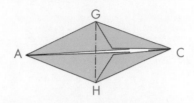

2 Fold point A to point C, unfold. In the crease just created, fold points B and D, lying inside on the right, outward to the left.

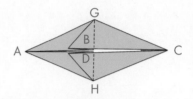

3 Valley fold at points B and D.

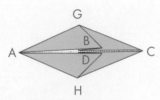

4 Mountain fold in the center crease.

5 Turn model. Pull point B to the right (see next illustration). Turn model, and repeat with point D. Turn.

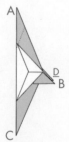

6 At point A, reverse fold inside.

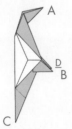

7 Reverse fold inside at points A and C.

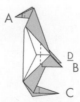

8 Form the beak by reverse folds inside and outside at point A. Valley fold at points B and D. Reverse fold inside at point C.

9 Completed Penguin.

BUTTERFLY

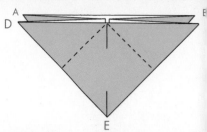

1 Start with Basic Form V. Valley fold in the dashed lines at points C and D.

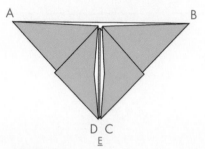

2 Turn over.

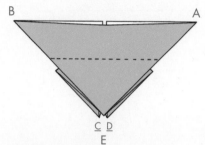

3 Valley fold in the dashed line to bring up points E, C, and D.

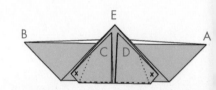

4 Fold points C and D down, at the same time pressing points X towards the center.

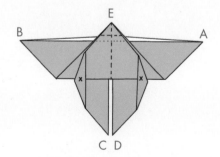

5 Mountain and valley fold at point E. Valley fold in the center crease.

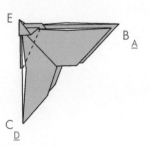

6 Valley fold in the dashed line in front and behind.

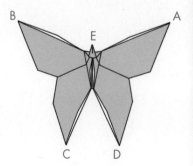

7 Completed Butterfly, as it unfolds.

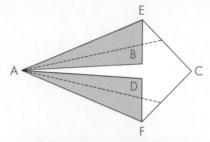

1 Start with Basic Form I, the Kite Fold. By valley folds in the dashed lines, bring the edges A–E and A–F to the center crease.

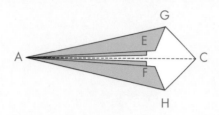

2 Valley fold in the center crease.

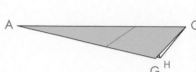

3 At point A, reverse fold inside in the dotted line.

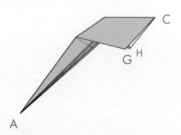

4 At point A, reverse fold toward the inside in the dotted line.

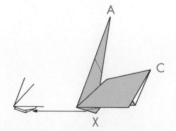

5 At point A, reverse fold in the dotted line toward the inside. By reverse fold to the inside, bring corner X into the inner part of the fold.

6 At point A, reverse fold toward the outside along the indicated line.

7 At point A, fashion the beak by reverse folds to the inside and outside. At point C, fashion the tail by reverse folds to the inside and the outside.

8 At point A, bend the beak down.

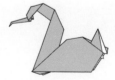

9 Completed Cormorant.

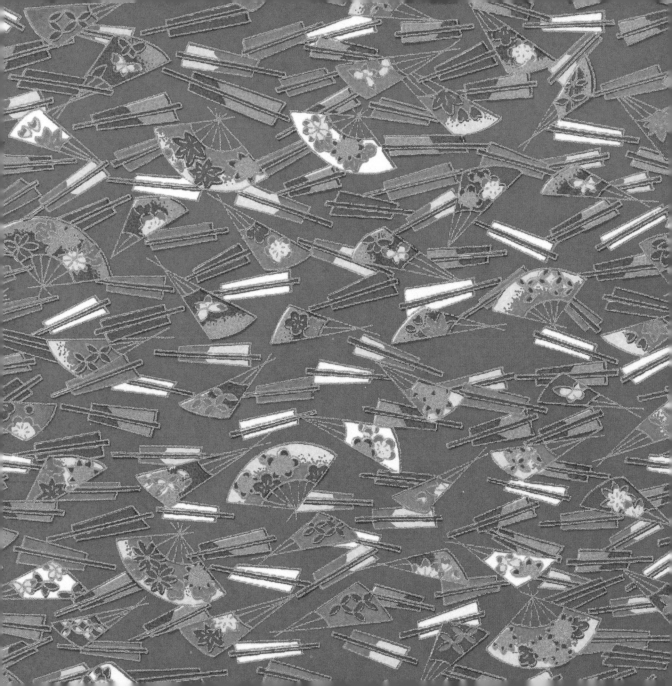

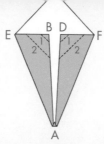

1 Start with Basic Form I, the Kite Fold. Fold point A, before folding the basic form, onto the folding sheet, so that it lies inside, as shown in the illustration. Valley fold in the dashed lines at corners B and D.

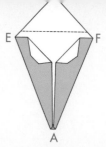

2 At corner C, valley fold in the dashed line.

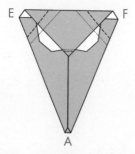

3 By mountain and valley folds, form the beak at corner C, and the ears at corners E and F.

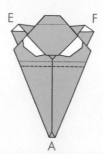

4 Mountain fold in the dotted line on top. Form the head by mountain and valley folds below the beak.

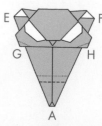

5 Mountain fold at corners G and H. Fashion the tail at point A by mountain and valley folds.

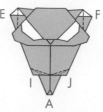

6 At corners I and J, form the feet by mountain and valley folds. At corners E and F, tuck the outer edges into the inner sides of the ears.

7 The completed Owl.

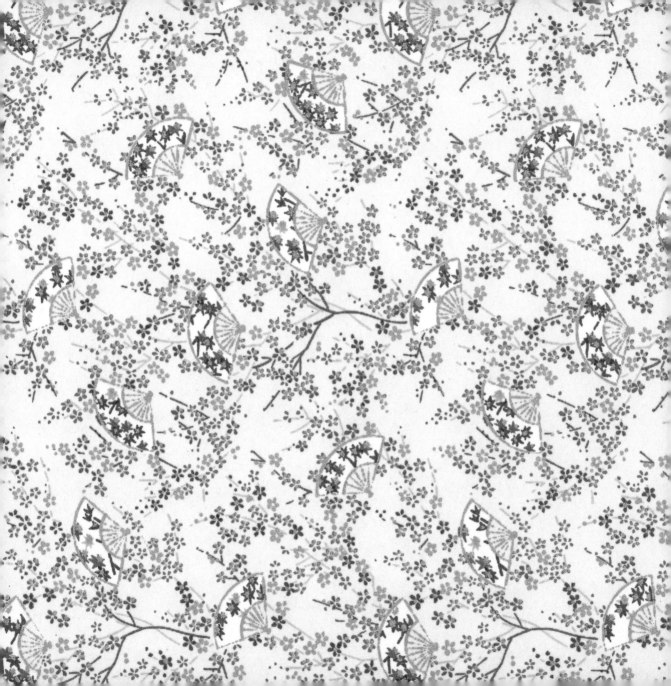

LAWN OR MARSH GRASS

1 Fold as if to make a book.

2 Fold over the bend in an upward direction.

3 Open the figure, press the middle bend flat, then change the valley fold on the reverse of the figure into a mountain fold.

4 Fold the figure together again, and crease the book as often as you like into an accordion shape.

5 Cut into the paper from the edges to make different blades or shapes of grass.

6 Open up the cut fold and bring the figure together as described in step 3.

BLADES OF GRASS

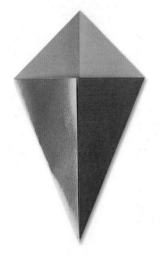

1 Make Basic Form I, the Kite Fold.

2 Repeat the folds of the Kite Fold in opposite directions.

3 Fold the two points on top of each other.

4 Fold the figure together in the middle.

5 Pull the point that is on the inside slightly toward the outside and firmly press the fold that appears at the bottom of the figure.

BUSH I

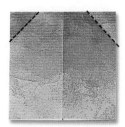

1 Fold paper vertically in the middle, as if to fold into a book. Unfold, and fold both sides towards the middle line.

2 Fold together in the middle, top to bottom, as shown above so that the folds are on the inside. On the dashed lines at the top of the bend, make the prefold for two sink folds.

3 Open the figure and fold all four side corners inward slightly diagonally as shown.

4 Close the figure while you push the sink folds inward. This is the finished Bush. To make bushes of different heights, fold the lower edges inward as high as you like. To make a group of bushes or an entire hedge, put several of these bushes together, overlapping them slightly, and perhaps glue them together.

BUSH II

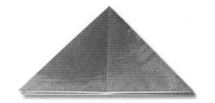

1 Start with Basic Form V.

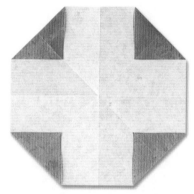

2 Open the form and fold all four corners slightly inward.

3 Next, fold the figure back into the shape of Basic Form V. On the dashed lines, make sink folds on all four wings of the figure.

4 Fold the wings to the side so that they point in all four directions. This is the finished Bush.

5 If you prefer a more closed shape Bush, you can add some glue to the wings on the inside, to stick them together. Then the Bush will not open so wide anymore.

TREE

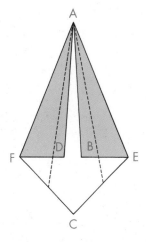

1 Start with Basic Form I, the Kite Fold. At point A, valley fold in the dashed lines.

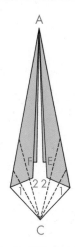

2 At point C, valley fold in the dashed lines 1 and 2.

3 Fold point C in the dashed line onto folding figure.

4 Valley fold in the center crease.

5 By reverse fold to the inside, fold the inside-lying point C sideways, outward.

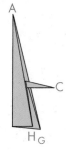

6 Completed Tree.

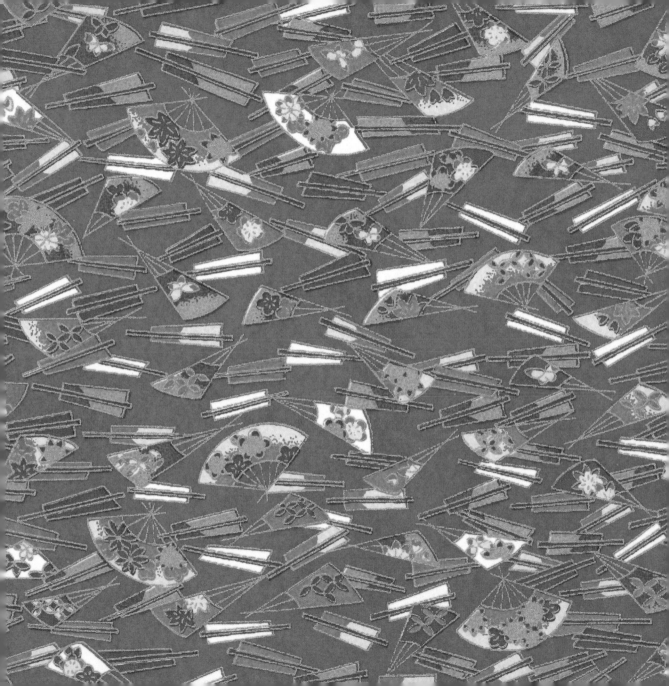

PALM TREE HEAD

1 Start with Basic Form III. Open folds.

2 Face paper wrong side up. Fold paper vertically in the middle. The opposite edges must lie one on top of the other.

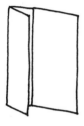

3 Open and fold both sides toward the middle line.

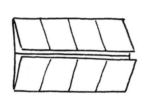

4 Repeat, but fold in a horizontal direction.

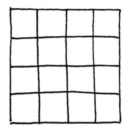

5 Open the fold. You should have 16 equally large squares.

6 Pull the sides and the corners of the figure upward by placing the double triangles at each of the small corners of the diagonals on top of each other.

7 Fold the lower and the upper edges onto the horizontal middle line so that both the right and left edges lie along the vertical middle line at the same time.

8 Turn the figure over. Fold a sink point by putting together the square in the middle of the form as shown, as if folding Basic Form V.

9 On the dashed line, fold a forward and a rear point to each side. Turn the figure over.

10 Secure Basic Form V with a little glue so that the figure won't spring open.

PALM TREE TRUNK

1 For the trunk, tightly roll a piece of paper diagonally and secure it with a little glue. The trunk's shape should be slightly wider as it goes down toward the ground.

2 Flatten the narrower tip of the trunk, add glue to hold, and position it into a wing from below as close as possible to the middle point of the Palm Tree Head.

FLOWER I

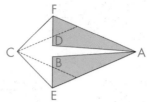

1 Start with Basic Form I, the Kite Fold. At corner C, valley fold in the dashed lines.

2 Valley fold in the dashed lines, outward to the right, the inside corners B and D.

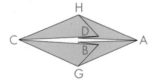

3 Turn the model over.

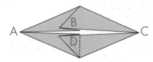

4 At point D, fashion the form of a kite by the indicated mountain and valley folds.

5 Valley fold at point D. Fold point B like D.

6 At points A and C, valley fold in the dashed lines.

7 By mountain and valley folds, bring points A and C into the position shown in the next illustration.

8 By mountain and valley folds in the lines indicated, bring points A and C flat onto the model's center.

9 Mountain fold in the dotted line at point A. Repeat at point C. Tuck points A and C under points B and D.

10 Completed Flower I.

FLOWER II

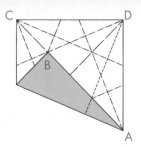

1 Fold Basic Form I, the Kite Fold, from all four corners of the paper and unfold again. Fold edge A–B in the existing crease to the center crease, then fold edge A–D in the existing crease to the center crease.

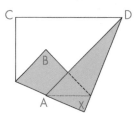

2 By a valley fold in the dashed line and a mountain fold in the dotted line, X falls onto the point shown in the next illustration.

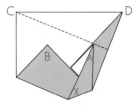

3 Fold in the existing crease edge C–D to the center crease.

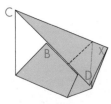

4 By a valley fold in the dashed line and a mountain fold in the dotted line, X falls onto the point shown in the next illustration.

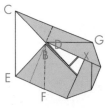

5 Fold edge B–E in the dotted line inwards under crease B–F. Simultaneously, fold point C onto corner G.

6 By means of a valley fold in the dashed line and a mountain fold in the dotted line, X falls onto the point shown in the next illustration.

7 By means of a valley fold in the dashed line and a mountain fold in the dotted line, X falls onto the point shown in the final illustration. Tuck point B under point A (shown in previous illustrations).

8 Completed Flower II.

TULIP HEAD

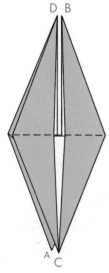

1 Start with Basic Form VII. Rotate the basic form. Fold upward point C in front, and point A in the back.

2 Valley fold right and left, in front and back, in the dashed lines. Valley fold at corner E, in the dashed-dotted line, and unfold again.

3 Press the tulip blossom open, from the center outward, and flatten out corner E.

4 The completed Tulip Head.

STEM WITH LEAF

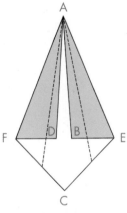

1 Start with Basic Form I, the Kite Fold. At point A, valley fold in the dashed lines.

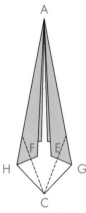

2 At point C, valley fold in the dashed lines.

3 Fold point C onto the model by a valley fold in the dashed line.

4 Mountain fold in the center crease.

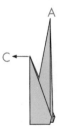

5 Pull point C—the leaf—lightly sideways, and crease again the changed lower creases.

TO ATTACH Glue Tulip Head to the stem.

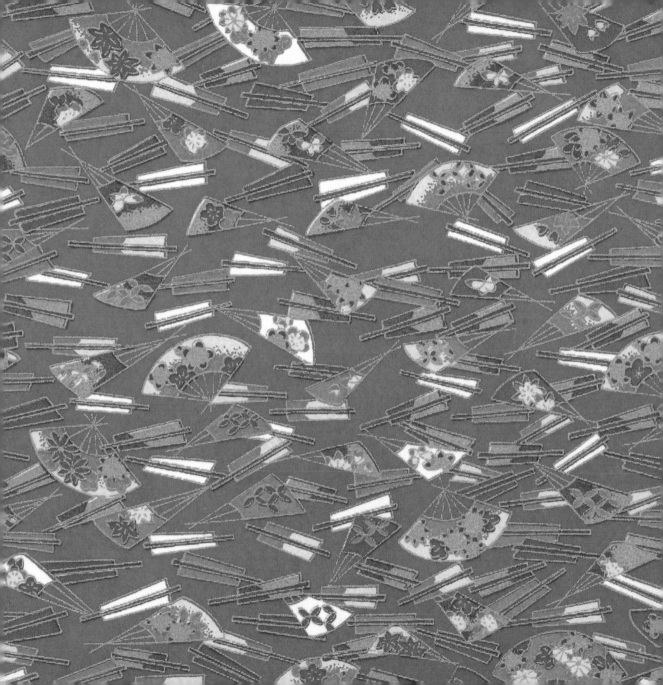

ROSE

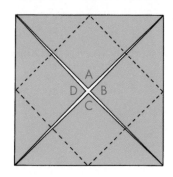

1 Start with Basic Form III. Once more, fold all corners to the center point.

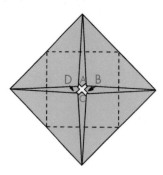

2 For a third time, fold all corners to the center point.

3 Turn over.

4 Again fold all corners to the center point.

5 Carefully pull forward, across corners E, F, G, and H, the corners lying on top in the center point, until they poke up.

6 Simultaneously, lightly press corners E, F, G, and H toward the outside; see enlarged illustration above.

7 After completing the work on the first four corners, also pull forward the four other corners in the back.

STEM WITH LEAF

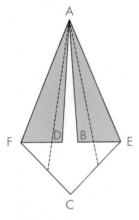

1 Start with Basic Form I, the Kite Fold. At point A, valley fold in the dashed lines.

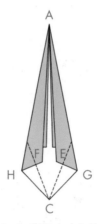

2 At point C, valley fold in the dashed lines.

3 Fold point C onto the model by a valley fold in the dashed line.

4 Mountain fold in the center crease.

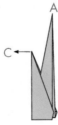

5 Pull point C—the leaf—lightly sideways, and crease again the changed lower creases.

TO ATTACH Glue Rose to the stem.

LILY

1 Begin with Basic Form VI.

2 With opening at the top of the model, fold left-upper corner to vertical midline. Unfold.

3 Place your index finger between layers of folded left-upper corner and move point A over to right side of model. Press to flatten.

4 Crease along dashed lines. Push left and right points of resulting triangle to center of model and press to flatten.

5 Turn model over and repeat Steps 2–4 for each side corner.

6 Fold bottom flap up. Repeat for each side.

7 Fold the right-upper layer to the left side and the left-lower layer to the right side.

8 Fold left and right upper corners to vertical midline.

9 Turn model over and repeat for each side.

10 One at a time, pull each petal downward and dot over the surface, using marking pen.

11 Open flower by pulling petals downward and curling them under, using the shaft of a ballpoint pen.

12 Completed Lily.

FOR STEM:

13 Insert one end of floral wire into the bottom of the lily. Wrap floral tape around the bottom point of the lily and continue wrapping downward around floral wire.

14 Apply a small amount of glue onto stem end of each silk flower pistil and stamen. Insert glued end into center of lily. Allow glue to dry.

DUCKLING

1 Make Basic Form I, the Kite Fold. If you want the Duckling to have a different colored bill, first fold a small corner backwards.

2 Turn the figure over.

3 Fold the upper point downward.

4 Turn the point upward one more time.

5 Fold the figure together in the middle. Then, as shown by the dashed line, form the neck with a reverse fold.

6 On the dashed line, form the head with a reverse fold.

7 Then, following the dashed lines, form the bill with a series of alternating mountain and valley folds. (You must turn the paper before each new fold to form an accordion type of fold.)

8 Carefully, pull the Duckling's tail in an upward direction and firmly press the new fold (crimp fold) together.

9 Then, as shown by the dashed line, fold the two lower edges toward the inside.

10 Completed Duckling.

MAMA DUCK

1 Make Basic Form I, the Kite Fold. If you want the Duckling to have a different colored bill, first fold a small corner backwards.

2 Turn the figure over.

3 Fold the upper point downward.

4 Turn the point upward one more time.

5 Fold the figure together in the middle. Then, as shown by the dashed line, form the neck with a reverse fold.

6 Following the dashed line, the head is then formed with a reverse fold. At the head, pull the reverse fold slightly in an upward direction and firmly press the new fold.

7 On the dashed lines, form the bill with an accordion fold and pull slightly downward. The Duck's tail is pulled in an upward direction. Fold the two lower edges of the figure upward.

8 On the dashed lines, fold the two wings downward again.

9 Completed Mama Duck.

JUMPING FROG

1 Start with Basic Form V.

2 Open the figure and then fold two corners toward the center. Undo the last step and return once more to the shape of the Basic Form V.

3 Turn the figure over and fold the Frog's legs toward the middle line.

4 On the dashed lines, fold the two legs outward once again.

5 Completed Step 4.

6 Turn the Frog over. If, shortly and firmly with your fingertip, you tap the very outer point of the rear of the Frog's head, the Frog will jump into the air!

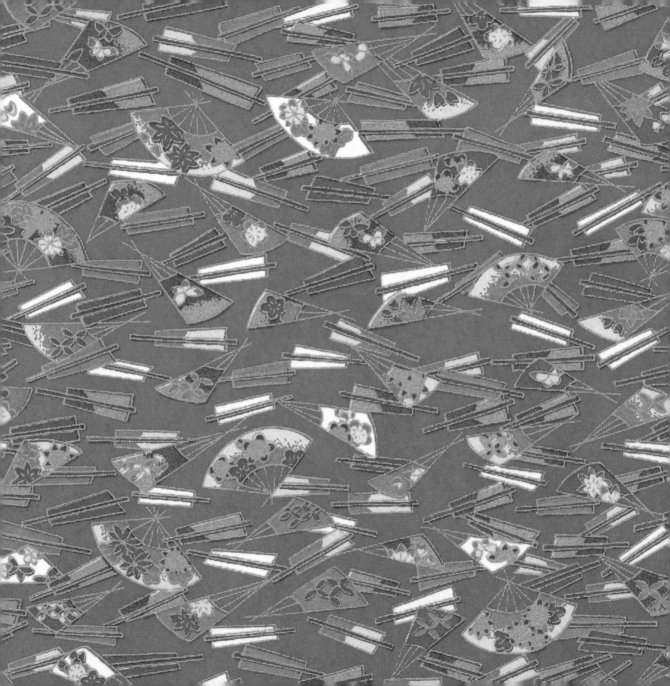

CAT HEAD

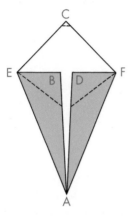

1 Start with Basic Form I, the Kite Fold. Valley fold at corners C, B, and D.

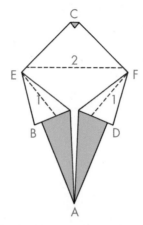

2 Valley fold in lines 1 at corners B and D, and in line 2 at corner C.

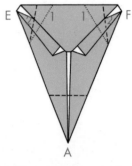

3 Valley fold at point A. Tuck point A under point C. Mountain fold at points E and F in the dotted lines, and valley fold in the dashed lines.

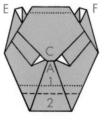

4 Mountain fold in the dotted line on top. Mountain and valley fold in lines 1 and 2.

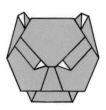

5 Finished Cat Head.

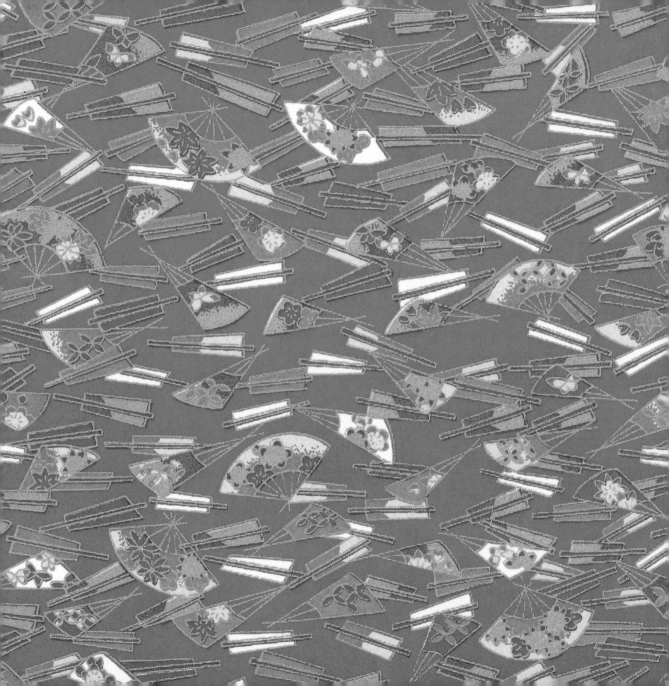

CAT BODY

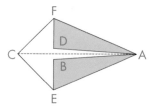

1 Start with Basic Form I, the Kite Fold. Valley fold in center crease.

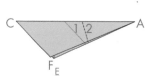

2 At point A, reverse fold inward and outward.

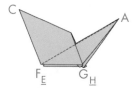

3 Bring corner G upward by valley fold in the dashed line A–F.

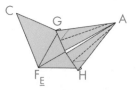

4 Valley folds at point A. By mountain folds in the dotted lines, G and H will fall on the points shown in the illustration with step 5.

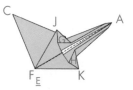

5 Valley fold in the tail's center crease, J onto K.

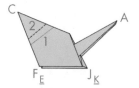

6 At point C, reverse fold inward and outward.

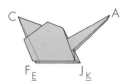

7 At point C, mountain fold in front and behind.

8 Finished body model.

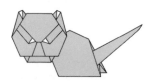

TO ATTACH Hang or glue the head to point C of the body.

HEN

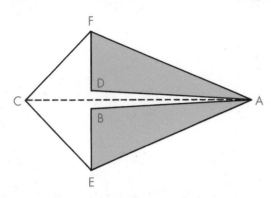

1 Start with Basic Form I, the Kite Fold. Valley fold in the center crease.

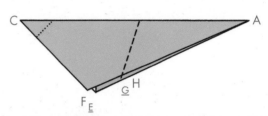

2 At point A, form the tail by reverse fold outward. At point C, fashion the beak by reverse fold to the inside.

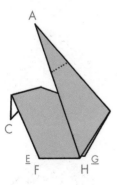

3 Reverse fold to the inside at point A. The chicken must stand on the edges E–F and F–H. If necessary, pull point A further over toward the head.

4 Cut out the Hen's red comb and glue it on.

ROOSTER

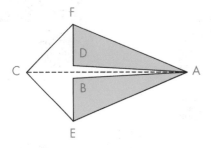

1 Start with Basic Form I, the Kite Fold. Valley fold in the center crease.

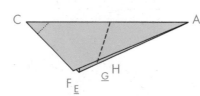

2 At point A, form the tail by reverse fold outward. At point C, fashion the beak by reverse fold to the inside.

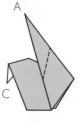

3 The folding sheet for the rooster can be somewhat larger than the one for the hen. At point A, reverse fold outward.

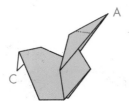

4 At point A, reverse fold to the inside.

5 Cut out the Rooster's red comb and glue it on.

RABBIT

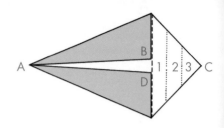

1 Start with Basic Form I, the Kite Fold. At corner C, valley fold in the dashed line, and mountain fold in the dotted lines. Corner C will now lie on the back side of the folding job.

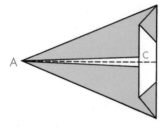

2 Valley fold in the center crease.

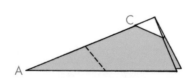

3 At point A, reverse fold outward.

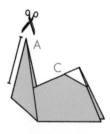

4 At point A, cut the ears open, and this very simple figure is finished.

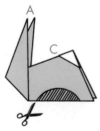

5 The Rabbit, however, can be refined a little bit. For this, cut out the hatched part, front and back.

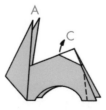

6 Lightly pull out point C. Valley folds in the dashed lines, front and back of the hind legs.

7 Completed Rabbit.

EASTER BUNNY PART I

1 Start with Basic Form VII. Inside reverse folds.

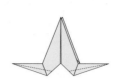

2 Valley fold both sides.

3 Valley fold in half, then rotate.

4 Outside reverse fold both layers together.

5 Outside reverse fold.

6 Pleat fold.

7 Outside reverse fold.

8 Cuts and valley open, both sides.

9 Mountain fold flaps.

10 Cut as shown.

11 Valley folds.

12 Pleat folds.

13 Pull and crimp into position.

14 Again, pull forward and squash fold.

15 Pull open ears.

16 Valley folds.

17 Inside reverse fold.

18 Completed part 1 (front) of Easter Bunny.

EASTER BUNNY PART II

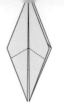

1 Start with Basic Form VII. Valley folds outward.

2 Turn over to other side.

3 Valley fold.

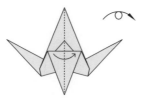

4 Valley fold in half, then rotate and turn over.

5 Inside reverse fold.

6 Outside reverse fold.

7 Tuck tip into center layers.

8 Outside reverse fold.

9 Inside reverse folds.

10 Inside reverse folds.

11 Completed part 2 (rear) of Easter Bunny.

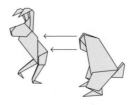

TO ATTACH Join parts 1 and 2 together as shown, and apply glue to hold.

Completed Easter Bunny shown with easter basket.

GREYHOUND PART I

1 Start with Base Fold III, valley fold.

2 Valley fold two layers, both sides.

3 Inside reverse fold.

4 Pleat folds, then outside reverse fold.

5 Outside reverse fold top layer only.

6 Inside reverse fold.

7 See close-up detail.

8 Pleat fold.

9 Cut to separate "ears," as shown.

10 Squash fold "ears."

11 Completed detail, to full view.

12 Inside reverse folds, for front "paws."

13 Cuts as shown.

14 Completed part 1 (front) of Greyhound.

GREYHOUND PART II

1 Start with Basic Form VII, valley fold, and repeat behind.

2 Inside reverse folds.

3 Valley fold.

4 Cuts as shown, then valley fold.

5 Valley fold.

6 Cuts as indicated.

7 Valley fold.

8 Squash folds.

9 Valley folds.

10 Valley folds. Then valley fold in half and rotate.

11 Valley fold.

12 Make cut as shown and mountain fold. Repeat behind.

13 Inside reverse fold "legs." Outside reverse "tail."

14 Inside reverse folds again.

15 Cut to form "tail."

16 Outside reverse folds to form back "paws."

17 Completed part 2 (rear) of Greyhound.

TO ATTACH Join parts 1 and 2 together per arrows, and glue to secure.

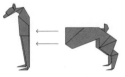

Completed Greyhound.

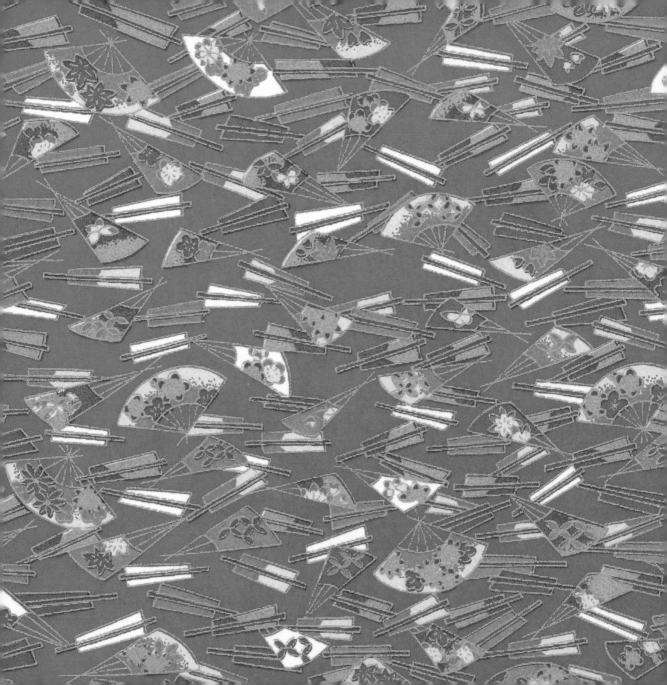

STANDING ELEPHANT

1 Make Basic Form I, the Kite Fold. Following the dashed lines fold both sides toward the middle line.

2 Turn the figure over. Fold the figure in the middle and turn it over again.

3 Completed Step 2.

4 Bring the top point toward the bottom. Fold the figure together in the middle.

5 Completed Step 4.

6 On the dashed line make a sink fold. Undo the sink fold again.

7 Along the dashed line make a sink fold, and pull the tip of the tail slightly upward.

8 On the dashed line, lay out the position of the head and the trunk with a sink fold.

9 Completed Step 8.

10 Fold the ears to the side on both sides of the figure.

11 Bring the ears backward again and firmly press them for a squash fold.

12 Open the trunk out into a diamond, and fold it as shown, making the lower part narrower.

13 Fold the trunk together again. On the dashed line form the trunk, shaping it with two sink folds.

14 Completed Standing Elephant.

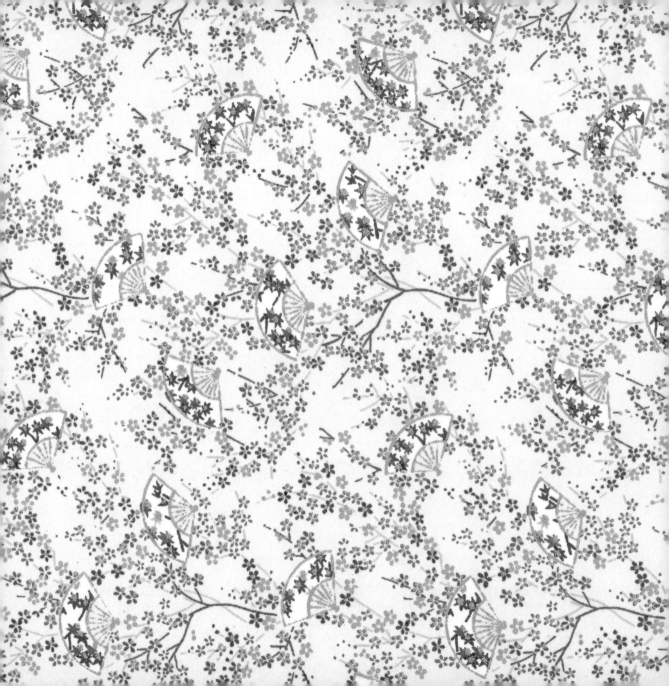

SITTING ELEPHANT

1 Make Basic Form I, the Kite Fold.

2 Fold the figure together in the middle. Along the dashed line, do a reverse fold.

3 Do another reverse fold as shown by the dashed line and you will form the back of the Elephant's head.

4 Now, along the dashed line fold the trunk downward with a sink fold.

5 Make another sink fold on the dashed line to move the trunk upward again.

6 Give the trunk its final shape with two reverse folds.

7 Now make a sink fold for the tail.

8 Fold the legs and ears forward.

9 Again, undo the folds and pull the tip of the tail upward. Fix it in position with a crimp fold, and also adjust the folds of the ears. Depending on how you like the position of the ears and forelegs and the angle of the Elephant's head, there are many possibilities.

SITTING BABY ELEPHANT

1 Make Basic Form VIII. The two tips point upward. Turn the figure over and, on the dashed lines, fold both sides in toward the middle.

2 For the head, make a series of mountain and valley folds that follow each other in an alternating pattern, as for an accordion fold, on the dashed lines.

3 Then turn the figure over and fold both tips outward for the ears.

4 Fold the figure together along the middle line so that the ears lie inward. On the dashed lines make sink folds.

5 At the head, fold a series of mountain and valley folds that follow each other in an alternating pattern, as for an accordion fold; pull the trunk upward slightly. On the three dashed lines make a sink fold for the foot and the trunk.

6 Then, on the dashed line, fold the body of the Elephant downward on both sides of the figure.

7 The ears are opened and pressed firmly as a squash fold.

BABY ELEPHANT PART 1

1 For the head, make Basic Form VIII. The two tips should point downward. Turn the figure over and, on the dashed lines, fold both sides to the middle line.

2 Again, following the dashed lines, make a mountain fold and then a valley fold, to create an accordion type of fold.

3 Fold the figure together as shown along the middle line so that the sections for the ears lie on top.

4 Pull the trunk upward a bit and, on the dashed line, bring the trunk upward again with a sink fold. Fold the ears forward and, on the other dashed line, make a reverse fold.

5 Fold the lower point, the neck, back along the dashed line with a reverse fold. On both other dashed lines form the trunk, using two sink folds.

6 Open the ears and firmly press them into squash folds.

BABY ELEPHANT PART II

1 Start with Basic Form III. Open folds.

2 Face paper wrong side up. Fold paper vertically in the middle. The opposite edges must lie one on top of the other.

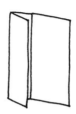

3 Open and fold both sides toward the middle line.

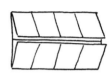

4 Repeat, but fold in a horizontal direction.

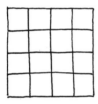

5 Open the fold. You should have 16 equally large squares.

6 Pull the sides and the corners of the figure upward by placing the double triangles at each of the small corners of the diagonals on top of each other.

7 Fold the lower and the upper edges onto the horizontal middle line so that both the right and left edges lie along the vertical middle line at the same time.

8 Fold the figure in the middle as shown, so that the open sides lie on the outside. Fold all four wings inward halfway, and open the prefolds again.

9 Firmly press all four wings into squash folds.

10 Open up the figure, and make a mountain fold and then a valley fold along the dashed lines to create an accordion.

11 Fold the figure together again and pull the left side downward slightly. Press the crimp fold down firmly. The toes of the Elephant come from a mountain fold, valley fold, and mountain fold again, made on the dashed lines.

TO ATTACH Glue or paste the head piece onto the body as shown so that the end of the back point is seen as only a little tail.

RESTING OLD LION

1 Make Basic Form I, the Kite Fold. Following the dashed lines, fold both sides toward the middle line.

2 Turn the figure over. Fold the figure in the middle.

3 Turn the figure over.

4 Bring the top point toward the bottom.

5 Fold the figure together in the middle.

6 Pull the right point far enough upward so a piece of what will be the lion's paws can still be seen. On the dashed line make a sink fold. Undo the sink fold again.

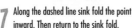

7 Along the dashed line sink fold the point inward. Then return to the sink fold.

8 On the dashed line make a small squash fold to form ears on both sides of the Lion figure.

9 Do a sink fold on the dashed line.

10 Make the Lion's tail narrower on both sides of the figure.

11 On the dashed line fold the tail upward using a sink fold.

12 Then, at the tip of the tail, make another sink fold on the dashed line and open the fold outward so that a diamond-shaped tuft appears at the end of the tail.

13 This is the Old Lion.

RESTING YOUNG LION

1 Make Basic Form I, the Kite Fold. Following the dashed lines, fold both sides toward the middle line.

2 Turn the figure over. Fold the figure in the middle.

3 Turn it over again.

4 Bring the top point toward the bottom.

5 Fold the figure together in the middle.

6 Pull the right point far enough upward so a piece of what will be the Lion's paws can still be seen.

7 Then, on the dashed lines make two reverse folds.

8 In this next dashed line fold the point inward.

9 Then, on the dashed line fold the corners of both sides of the figure outward.

10 Form tail with sink fold. Make the Lion's tail narrower on both sides of the figure.

11 On the dashed line fold the tail upward using a sink fold.

12 Then, at the tip of the tail, make another sink fold on the dashed line and open the fold outward so that a diamond-shaped tuft appears at the end of the tail.

13 Completed Young Lion.

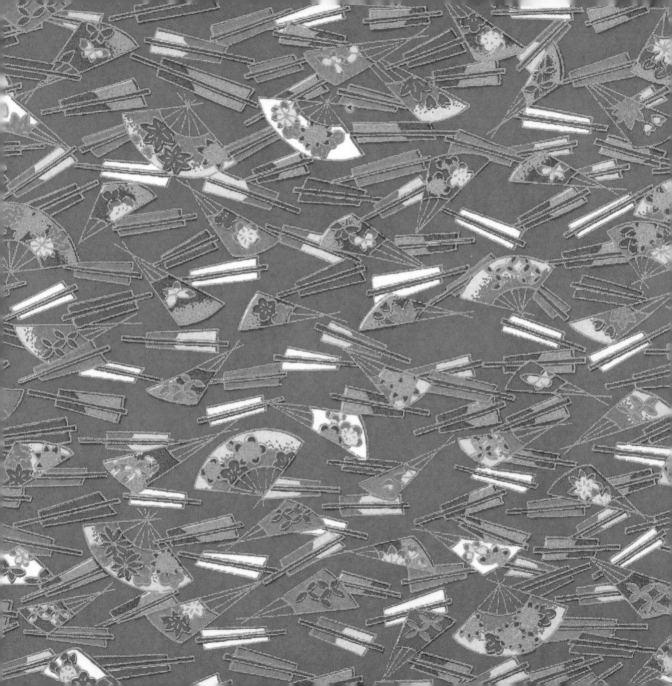

LITTLE LION PART I

1 Start with Basic Form VIII.

2 Open the figure and fold the two small corners inward.

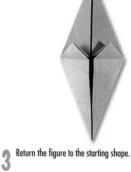

3 Return the figure to the starting shape.

4 Fold the figure together in the middle. Then, on the dashed line, make a sink fold.

5 Push this fold down from top to bottom so that the Lion's tail stands up vertically.

6 With a sink fold, prefold the tuft of the tail, then fold it back into a diamond shape. This is the body of the Lion cub.

LITTLE LION PART II

1 Face colored side of paper up. Fold diagonally.

2 Fold the two points along the edges downward. On the dashed line, fold the small point in a downward direction.

3 Completed Step 2.

4 Alongside this corner, fold the two small corners upward again.

5 Turn the figure over. Then, on the dashed lines, fold the corners upward so that the nose of the Lion appears. The tips of the ears are slightly folded inward.

6 Complete Lion's head (Little Lion, Part II).

TO ATTACH Glue the head to the body at any angle you wish.

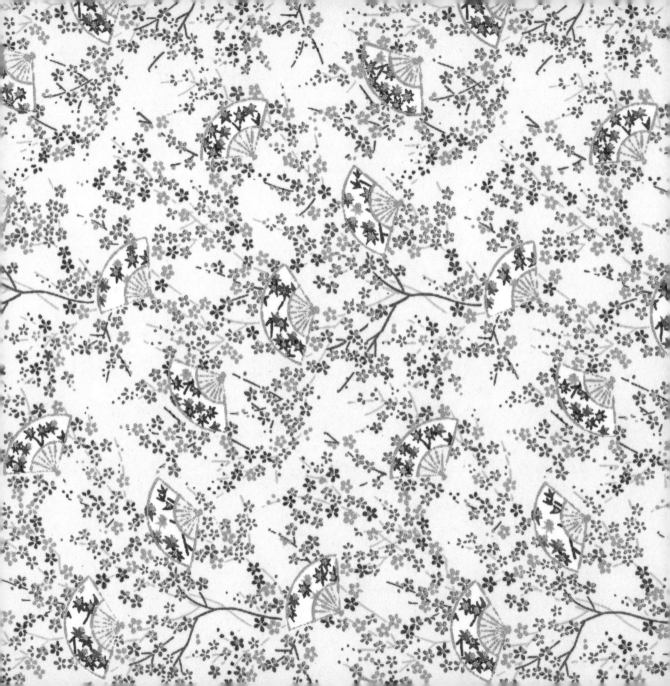

LITTLE TIGER PART I

1 Start with Basic Form VIII. Open out the form and fold the small corners outward.

2 Return your figure to the folds of Basic Form VIII. The Little Tiger now has white paws. Turn the figure over. On the dashed line prefold the tail.

3 Then fold it together along the line as shown, somewhat similar to an accordion-shaped fold.

4 Next fold the tip of the tail in an upward direction. Press the two little triangles of the tip of the tail together slightly so that the tip stands out backward a little bit.

5 Completed Little Tiger Part I (body).

LITTLE TIGER PART II

1 Face colored side of paper up. Fold diagonally.

2 Fold the two points along the edges downward. On the dashed line fold the small point in a downward direction.

3 Completed Step 2.

4 Alongside this corner fold the two small corners upward again.

5 Turn the figure over. Then, on the dashed lines, fold the corners upward so that the nose of the Tiger appears.

6 Complete Tiger's head (Little Tiger, Part II).

TO ATTACH Glue the head to the body at any angle you wish.

BABY GIRAFFE

1 Start with Basic Form VII. Turn the figure like this, so that the open points lie on top. On the dashed line fold both sides to the middle line.

2 Turn the figure over, and repeat this fold on the reverse side. On the dashed line fold the left wing of the figure downward. To do that, you need to first open the left wing and, after making the fold, close it again.

3 Then, on the dashed line, form the Giraffe's neck with a sink fold.

4 On the dashed line, fold and unfold the triangle on the back of the Giraffe on both sides of the figure. Pull the hind leg a little to the right. Seen from above, a small diamond now appears on the back.

5 Following the dashed line, form the Giraffe's head with a reverse fold. Fold the tip of the nose inward. Fold the corners on the back side of the head downward on both sides of the figure as ears.

6 On the dashed line, fold both forelegs slightly outward so that the Giraffe's front legs go into a light split. The Baby Giraffe stands very well on its three legs. But if you'd prefer four legs, just cut into the hind legs along the center crease to make one more.

GIRAFFE PART I

1 Start with Basic Form VIII. Fold the small wings back in an upward direction. Turn the figure over and, along the dashed line, fold the two upper edges to the middle line.

2 Now, fold the figure together along the middle line, and bring the small wings downward.

3 On the dashed line, form the Giraffe's head with a reverse fold.

4 Then, following the dashed line, fold the head point back with a reverse fold.

5 Bring the ears upward and then, on the dashed line, fold the Giraffe's mane.

6 The ears are again folded downward and slightly opened. Cut into the point for the horns up to the back of the head, and fold the horns outward. Again, following the dashed line, make a sink fold.

7 Fold the leftover point inward as shown so that it disappears entirely into the Giraffe's neck.

GIRAFFE PART II

1 For the Giraffe's body, make Basic Form VIII. Fold together so that both small wings are on the outside. On the dashed line fold the hind legs of the Giraffe with a sink fold.

2 Fold both wings back and then, as shown by the dashed line, form the forelegs with a sink fold.

3 Completed Step 2.

4 Bring the sink fold of the forelegs back and outward.

5 Now, fold the wings forward and then fold the points of the legs slightly inward. This way the Giraffe can stand freely. Cut into the legs along the bend, and push the four legs slightly outward.

TO ATTACH Now, put the head section into the body. Insert the neck in a straight line to the forelegs and the Giraffe will stand very securely. Because of the somewhat longer forelegs, it is well balanced despite being top-heavy. Glue the head and the body together and, at the same time, fold the wings on the body around the Giraffe's neck.

PANDA PART 1

1 Fold the paper for the body twice diagonally in the middle. The colored side lies inside.

2 Open the figure, and bring one corner to ... ...shed line bring

4 Close the figure diagonally.

5 On the dashed line fold the edges on both sides of the figure outward.

6 Then, on the dashed line turn the small corners on both sides of the figure inward.

7 That is the body of the Big Panda.

PANDA PART II

1 Fold the paper for the head diagonally in the middle. The colored side faces up.

2 Bring both points along the edges in a downward direction. Along the dashed line fold a small corner downward.

3 Completed Step 2.

4 Then, along this corner, both points are folded upward once more.

5 Turn the figure over and, on the dashed line, fold the lower corner upward.

6 Then, undo this fold, and on the dashed line fold the lower corner upward. Cut the eye rings in along this fold.

7 Undo all other folds again by opening up the figure. Fold the paper in the other diagonal direction.

8 Cut out a slight half-cross-shaped piece. Refold the figure, as you did before, and then fold the small white corner between the ears towards the back.

9 Fold the points of the ears inward and the tip of the nose upward. That is the head of Panda.

TO ATTACH Paste the head onto the body at any angle.

LITTLE PANDA PART I

1 Start with paper colored side face up. Make the Basic Form V.

2 Open the form, and fold the two lower corners to the middle.

3 Undo this fold again and bring half of both lower sides inward.

4 Fold both diagonal edges inward.

5 Refold the figure once again into the shape of Basic Form V.

6 Open the back triangle of the form by laying it out into a square on the left side of the figure.

7 Fold the left, upper corner forward up to the point of the black corner.

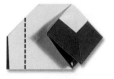

8 Open this fold once more and make a sink fold on this preliminary crease. On the dashed line, fold the back edges to the front on both sides of the figure.

9 This is the body of Little Panda.

LITTLE PANDA PART II

1 Fold the paper for the head diagonally in the middle. The colored side faces up.

2 Bring both points along the edges in a downward direction. Along the dashed line fold a small corner downward.

3 Completed Step 2.

4 Then, along this corner, both points are folded upward once more.

5 Turn the figure over and, on the dashed line, fold the lower corner upward.

6 Then, undo this fold, and on the dashed line fold the lower corner upward.

7 Cut the eye rings in along this fold.

8 Undo all other folds again by opening up the figure. Fold the paper in the other diagonal direction.

9 Cut out a slight half-cross-shaped piece. Refold the figure, as you did before, and then fold the small white corner between the ears towards the back.

10 Fold the points of the ears inward and the tip of the nose upward. That is the head of Panda.

TO ATTACH Paste the head onto the body at any angle.

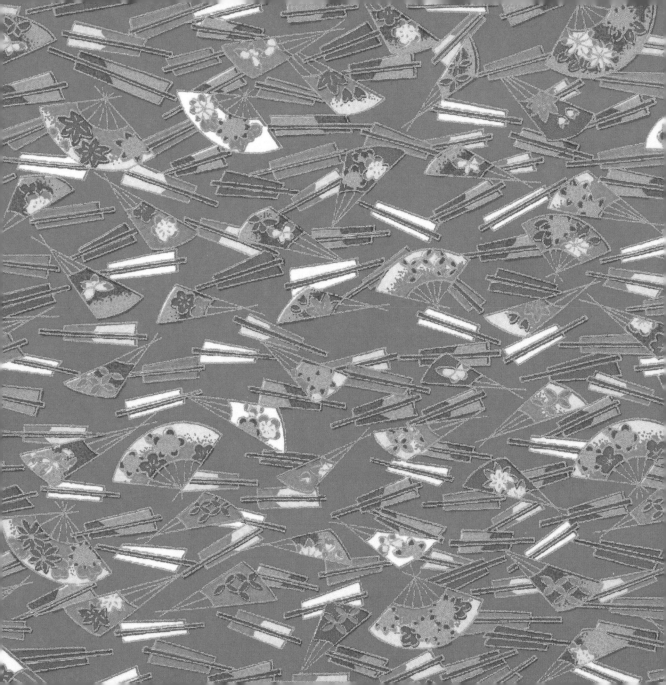

MOTHER BEAR PART I

1 Start with Basic Form III. Open folds.

2 Face paper wrong side up. Fold paper vertically in the middle. The opposite edges must lie one on top of the other.

3 Open and fold both sides toward the middle line.

4 Repeat, but fold in a horizontal direction.

5 Open the fold. You should have 16 equally large squares.

6 Pull the sides and the corners of the figure upward by placing the double triangles at each of the small corners of the diagonals on top of each other.

7 Fold the lower and the upper edges onto the horizontal middle line so that both right and left edges lie along the vertical middle line at the same time.

8 Fold the two right wings to the left side and, on the dashed lines, fold these two wings inward. These are the front legs of the Bear.

9 Now, along the dashed lines, fold the hind legs outward.

10 Fold the Bear's body together in the middle.

11 Make a small sink fold on the back.

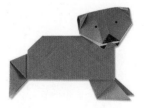

12 Completed part I of Mother Bear, shown with Part II (head) attached.

MOTHER BEAR PART II

1 Fold the paper for the head of Mother Bear diagonally in the middle twice. Fold and unfold the paper on both dashed lines.

2 Fold in the right and left corners up to the creases, and close the figure in the middle.

3 For the ears, bring the corners down on the dashed lines, and turn the corner upward for the nose.

4 Open the ears into Squash Folds, but don't press them entirely flat. Bend the ears slightly forward. Bring the triangled back of the snout forward as shown so that it is not completely hidden by the front part. Fold both halves of the head slightly rearward along the bridge of the nose so that the head becomes more pliant.

TO ATTACH Glue the back of the head, at any angle you wish, to one side of the Bear's body. At the same time, make sure that the Bear's head is not pressed flat again!

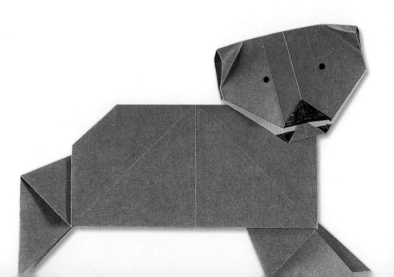

BEAR CUB PART I

1 Start with Basic Form V. Fold both upper-lying wings to the middle line, and then undo the prefolds again.

2 Crease the left, upper wing up to the prefold. Open this crease and firmly press the fold into a squash fold.

3 On the dashed lines fold the back-paw point that appears upward. Bring a small corner inward and fold the paw downward again.

4 Completed Step 3.

5 Repeat steps 2 to 3 with the right wing on the back of the figure. Fold the wing of the Basic Form V to the side so that you can make the forelegs.

6 Fold the right wing to the middle line. Open this wing and fold the point inward along the dashed line. On the dashed line, fold the front paw upward and then again downward. Make the left foreleg in the same way, and set up the figure so that the front paws lie flat on the ground.

BEAR CUB PART II

1 Fold the paper for the head of Bear Cub diagonally in the middle twice. Both corners are simply folded inward up to the middle line. Fold the figure together in the middle.

2 Fold in the right and left corners up to the creases, and close the figure in the middle.

3 For the ears, bring the corners down on the dashed lines, and turn the corner upward for the nose.

4 Open the ears into squash folds, but don't press them entirely flat. Bend the ears slightly forward. Bring the triangled back of the snout forward as shown so that it is not completely hidden by the front part. Fold both halves of the head slightly rearward along the bridge of the nose so that the head becomes more pliant.

TO ATTACH Attach the head of the Bear Cub at any angle you wish to one of the front legs of the body.

GORILLA PART 1

1 Start with square sheet cut diagonally, then valley fold.

2 Inside reverse folds.

3 Valley folds.

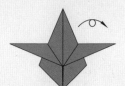

4 Turn over to other side.

5 Valley folds and squash folds.

6 Pleat fold.

7 Squash folds.

8 Valley fold.

9 Valley fold.

10 Mountain fold.

11 Valley fold.

12 Cut as shown.

13 Make cuts as shown.

14 Inside reverse folds.

15 Outside reverse folds.

16 Valley folds.

17 Mountain fold in half.

18 Pull and crimp head into position.

19 Pull and crimp open.

20 Unfold in direction of arrow.

21 Valley fold both sides to extend arms.

22 Completed part 1 (top) of Gorilla.

GORILLA PART II

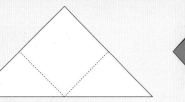

1 Start with square sheet cut diagonally, then valley fold.

2 Inside reverse folds.

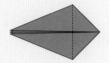

3 Valley fold.

4 Turn over to other side.

5 Valley fold.

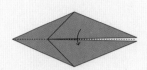

6 Valley fold in half.

7 Valley fold both front and back.

8 Mountain fold both front and back.

9 Repeat.

10 Inside reverse fold.

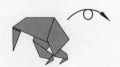

11 Cut as shown and rotate.

12 Completed part 2 (rear) of gorilla.

TO ATTACH

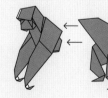

1 Join the two parts together as shown and apply glue to hold.

2 Completed Gorilla.

ZEBRA PART I

1 Start with Basic Form VII. Pleat fold.

2 Valley fold.

3 Pull and crimp fold as shown, then rotate.

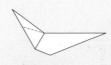

4 Inside reverse fold.

5 Valley fold.

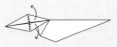

6 Make cuts then valley unfold.

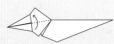

7 Valley fold.

8 Outside reverse fold.

9 Pull some paper out from inside.

10 Valley fold both front and back.

11 Make cut as shown.

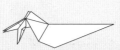

12 Valley fold both front and back.

13 Inside reverse fold.

14 Inside reverse fold.

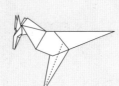

15 Valley fold both sides.

16 Pleat and crimp fold.

17 Turn over to other side.

18 Inside reverse fold.

19 Valley fold both sides.

20 Pleat and crimp.

21 Make cuts into mane, and add pattern.

22 Completed part 1 (front) of Zebra.

ZEBRA PART II

1 Start with Basic Form VII. Valley fold.

2 Turn over.

3 Cuts as shown.

4 Valley folds.

5 Cuts and mountain folds.

6 Turn over to other side.

7 Valley fold.

8 Valley fold in half and rotate.

9 Valley fold, and mountain fold both sides.

10 Inside reverse fold.

11 Inside reverse fold.

12 Turn over to other side.

13 Valley fold.

14 Inside reverse folds.

15 Inside reverse fold.

16 Valley fold to both sides.

17 Squash fold tail, and add pattern.

18 Completed part 2 (rear) of Zebra.

TO ATTACH Join both parts together and apply glue to hold.

GAZELLE PART I

1 Start with Basic Form VII. Valley fold.

2 Cut as shown.

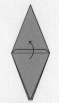

3 Valley fold.

4 Valley folds both sides.

5 Valley fold and rotate.

6 Outside reverse fold.

7 Outside reverse fold.

8 Inside reverse fold.

9 Vertical cut through, then make side cuts and valley unfold both sides.

10 Cut as shown.

11 Valley fold.

12 Valley fold back.

13 Valley fold both sides.

14 Tuck "horns" in between head layers.

15 Inside reverse folds.

16 Valley fold.

17 Turn over to other side.

18 Inside reverse fold.

19 Valley fold.

20 Valley fold and crimp into position. Add coloring.

21 Completed part 1 (front) of Gazelle.

GAZELLE PART II

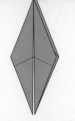

1 Start with Basic Form VII. Valley folds.

2 Turn over to other side.

3 Valley fold.

4 Valley fold.

5 Valley folds.

6 Valley fold in half.

7 Rotate.

8 Outside reverse fold.

9 Inside reverse folds, both sides.

10 Repeat.

11 Completed part 2 (rear) of Gazelle.

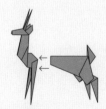

TO ATTACH Join part 1 (front) of Gazelle and part 2 (rear) together. Apply glue to hold, and add body coloring.

WATER BUFFALO PART I

1 Start with Basic Form VII. Valley fold.

2 Rotate.

3 Outside reverse fold.

4 Pleat fold.

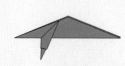

5 Outside reverse fold.

6 Inside reverse fold.

7 Make cuts as shown.

8 Mountain fold both sides.

9 Make cuts as shown.

10 Valley fold both sides.

11 Mountain fold both sides.

12 Valley fold both sides.

13 Inside reverse folds.

14 Valley fold both sides.

15 Valley fold both sides.

16 Repeat.

17 Outside reverse folds.

18 Valley fold then unfold.

19 Completed part I (front) of Water Buffalo.

WATER BUFFALO PART II

1 Start with Basic Form VII. Valley fold.

2 Valley fold and rotate.

3 Make cuts to the first layer on both sides, then valley unfold.

4 Outside reverse folds.

5 Mountain fold both sides.

6 Valley folds.

7 Crimp fold legs into place, both sides.

8 Inside reverse fold.

9 Valley folds to tail, mountain fold body inward.

10 Outside reverse folds.

11 Outside reverse fold.

12 Completed part II (rear) of Water Buffalo.

TO ATTACH:

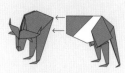

1 Join both parts together and apply glue to hold.

2 Valley fold.

3 Mountain fold, to give tail "life."

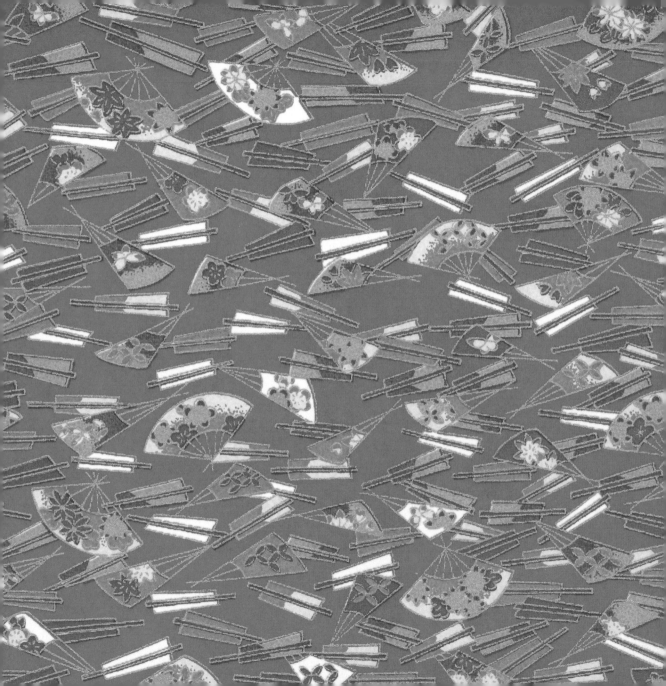

HIPPOPOTAMUS PART I

1 Start with Basic Form VII. Inside reverse folds.

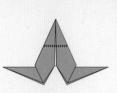

2 Cuts as shown.

3 Inside reverse folds.

4 Squash folds to front.

5 Valley folds.

6 Valley fold top layers and crimp feet outward.

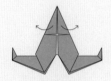

7 Open out as shown.

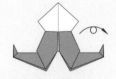

8 Valley in half, then rotate.

9 Pleat fold.

10 Unfold folds.

11 Pleat fold.

12 Pleat fold.

13 Outside reverse fold.

14 Cut as shown.

15 Outside reverse fold.

16 Squash fold ears forward.

17 Completed part I (front) of Hippopotamus.

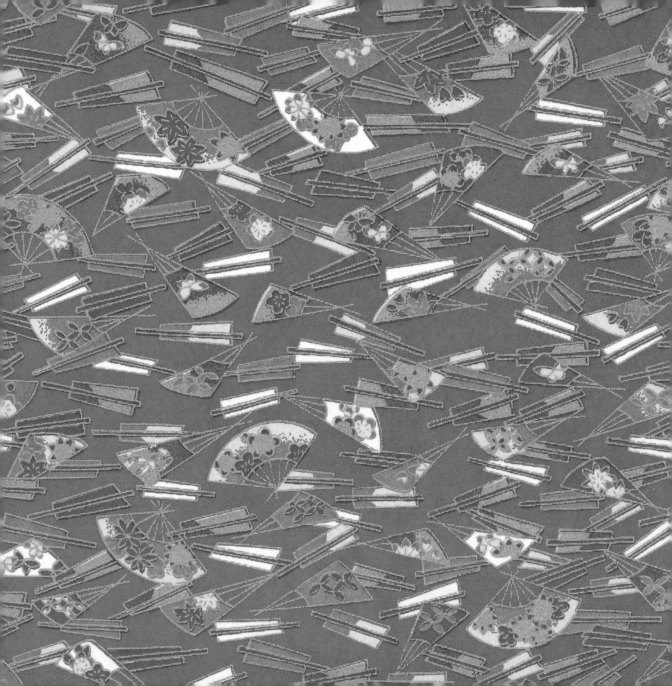

HIPPOPOTAMUS PART II

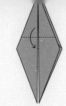

1 Start with Basic Form VII. Valley fold.

2 Turn over.

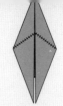

3 Cuts as shown.

4 Valley folds.

5 Mountain fold in half.

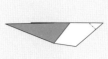

6 Rotate.

7 Inside reverse fold.

8 Valley fold both front and back.

9 Inside reverse fold.

10 Valley fold both sides.

11 Secure tail behind layers.

12 Cut as shown.

13 Inside reverse folds.

14 Inside reverse folds and rotate.

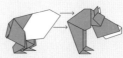

15 Completed part II (rear) of Hippopotamus.

TO ATTACH

Join both parts together as shown and apply glue to hold.

MOSQUITO PART I

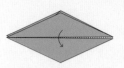

1 Start with Basic Form VII, then valley fold both sides.

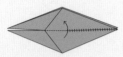

2 Cut through, then valley fold both sides.

3 Valley folds to center.

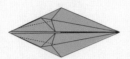

4 Valley folds.

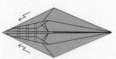

5 Pleat folds.

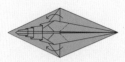

6 Mountain fold center sections out to sides. Valley fold outside flaps to left as shown.

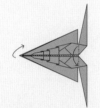

7 Mountain fold legs. Flip back flap to right as shown. Valley fold in half.

8 Pleat fold.

9 Inside reverse fold.

10 Pleat fold.

11 Valley folds both sides.

12 Outside reverse fold.

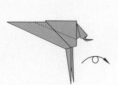

13 Valley fold, then turn over.

14 Valley fold.

15 Valley folds both sides.

16 Complete part I (top) of Mosquito.

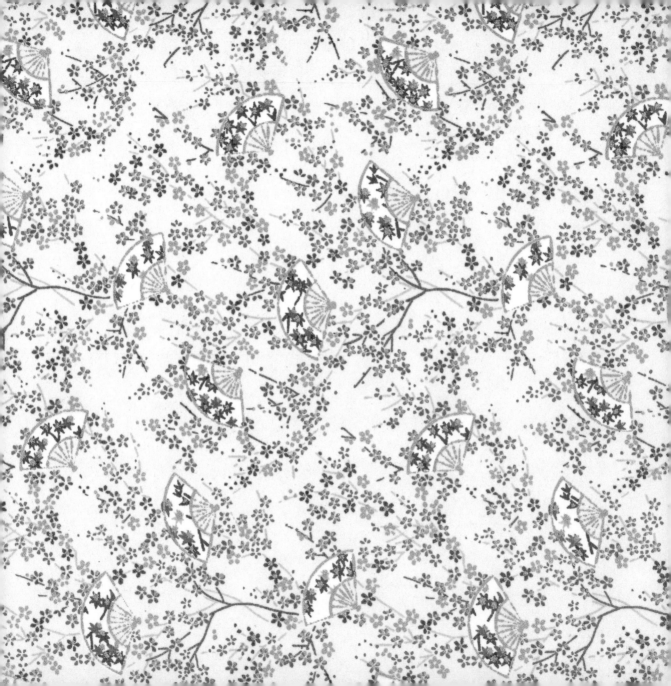

MOSQUITO PART II

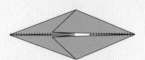

1 Start with Basic Form V, then cut as shown.

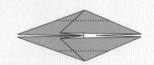

2 Valley folds.

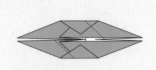

3 Valley folds.

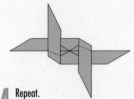

4 Repeat.

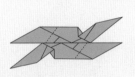

5 Valley folds.

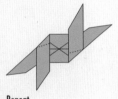

6 Repeat.

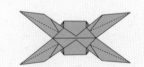

7 Squash folds.

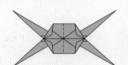

8 Mountain fold in half.

9 Completed part II (leg section) of Mosquito.

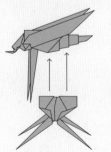

TO ATTACH Join parts I and II together as shown. Apply glue to hold.

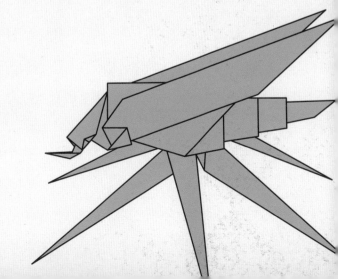

GECKO PART I

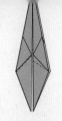

1 Start with Basic Form VII. Valley fold.

2 Inside reverse folds both right and left.

3 Valley folds.

4 Inside reverse folds.

5 Inside reverse folds.

6 Mountain folds.

7 Make cuts (3 on each foot).

8 Mountain fold outer "toes."

9 Repeat mountain folds.

10 Mountain folds again.

11 Mountain fold, front and back.

12 Valley folds.

13 Turn over to the other side.

14 Mountain folds.

15 Valley fold in half and rotate.

16 Pleat fold.

17 Inside reverse fold.

18 Valley folds.

19 Pull open mouth and crimp lower jaw into position.

20 Valley fold "toes."

21 Completed part I (front) of Gecko.

GECKO PART II

1 Start with Basic Form VII.

2 Cut, then turn over.

3 Mountain folds.

4 Inside reverse folds.

5 Mountain folds.

6 Turn over to other side.

7 Valley folds and squash folds at same time.

8 Turn over.

9 Mountain folds.

10 Squash folds.

11 Make cuts (3 on each foot) as shown.

12 Mountain fold "toes."

13 Completed part II (rear) of Gecko.

TO ATTACH

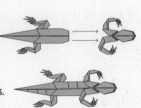

1 Join parts I (front) and II (rear) of Gecko together. Apply glue to hold.

2 Pleat fold left and right sides.

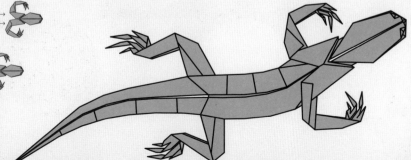

ALLIGATOR PART I

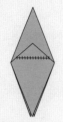

1 Start with Basic Form VII. Valley fold.

2 Cut as shown.

3 Valley fold.

4 Inside reverse folds.

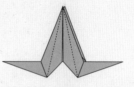

5 Valley fold both sides.

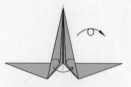

6 Valley fold in half and rotate.

7 Outside reverse fold.

8 Repeat.

9 Pull and squash fold open.

10 Inside reverse fold both sides.

11 Inside reverse fold both sides and lower jaw.

12 Outside reverse fold both sides.

13 Outside reverse folds for mouth.

14 Completed part I (front) of Alligator.

ALLIGATOR PART II

1 Start with Basic Form VII. Valley folds.

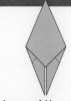

2 Inside reverse folds.

3 Cut as shown and valley fold.

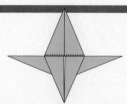

4 Make cuts to front layer only.

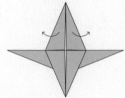

5 Valley folds.

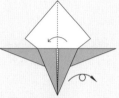

6 Valley fold and rotate.

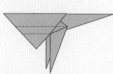

7 Mountain fold and valley fold under both sides.

8 Inside reverse fold both sides.

9 Inside reverse fold both sides, then pull and squash fold tail into position.

10 Inside reverse fold both front and back.

11 Valley fold both front and back.

12 Mountain fold both front and back.

13 Mountain fold both front and back.

14 Completed part II (rear) of Alligator.

TO ATTACH

Join parts I and II together as shown and apply glue to hold. Press and pull the tail into a natural-looking curve.

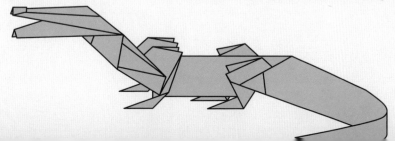

WILD DUCK

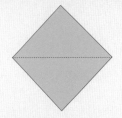

1 Valley fold square in half, diagonally.

2 Valley fold to half of baseline, front and back.

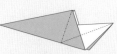

3 Valley fold front and back, and squash fold as you go.

4 Cuts as shown.

5 Now mountain folds.

6 Inside reverse fold.

7 Another inside reverse fold.

8 Inside reverse fold again.

9 Valley fold front and back.

10 Mountain fold, to form "tail" end.

11 Outside reverse fold.

12 Outside reverse fold.

13 Outside reverse fold.

14 Completed fold; see close-ups for head detail.

15 Pull to sides and flatten.

16 Pleat fold.

17 Return to full view.

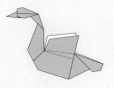

18 Pleat fold "wings" front and back.

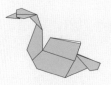

19 Completed Wild Duck.

RHINOCEROS PART I

1 Start with Basic Form VII, inside reverse folds.

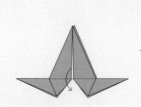

2 Valley fold.

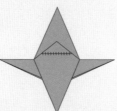

3 Cut off corner as indicated.

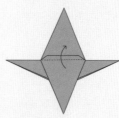

4 Valley fold.

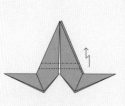

5 Pleat fold both layers together.

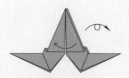

6 Valley fold in half, then rotate form.

7 Unfold pleat. Pull in direction of arrow.

8 Pleat fold at top, inside reverse folds at bottom.

9 Pleat fold at top, inside reverse folds for front "feet."

10 Pleat fold top layer only.

11 Cut apart as shown, then valley fold top layer.

12 Inside reverse fold, then see close-ups.

13 Inside reverse fold to shape "horn," squash folds for "ears."

14 Completed head detail of Rhinoceros.

15 Completed part I (front) of Rhinoceros.

RHINOCEROS PART II

1 Start with Basic Form VII. Valley fold each side.

2 Inside reverse fold.

3 Valley fold.

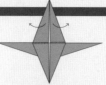

4 Cut as shown, then unfold in direction of arrows.

5 Valley folds.

6 Valley fold.

7 Valley folds, then squash folds as indicated.

8 Valley fold in half, then rotate form.

9 Cut as shown, then mountain fold front and back.

10 Inside reverse fold.

11 Valley fold front and back.

12 Inside reverse folds.

13 Inside reverse fold "legs."

14 Inside reverse fold "tail."

15 Outside reverse fold for "tail" tip.

16 Valley fold layers together. Glue to secure.

17 Inside reverse folds on "feet."

18 Completed part II (rear) of Rhinoceros.

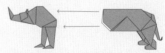

TO ATTACH Attach Rhinoceros parts I and II as shown; apply glue to hold.

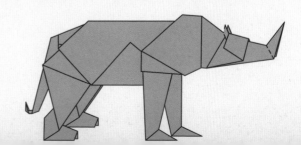

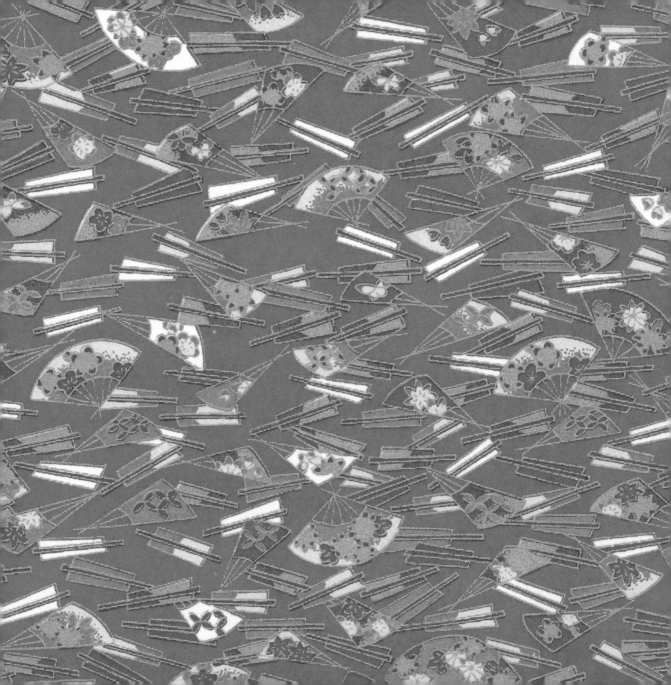

MAMA PENGUIN

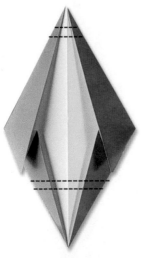

1 Make the Basic Form VIII, but do it a little differently, so the edges aren't all lying right along the middle line. Then, following the dashed line, make an inside crimp fold to form the beak.

2 Fold the figure together in the middle and, on the dashed line, fold the point into a backward sink fold.

3 Then, on the dashed line, the point of the foot is brought back to the front with another sink fold and the head is shaped with a reverse fold. Push the tips of the feet a little to flatten them.

4 Complete Mama Penguin.

PAPA PENGUIN

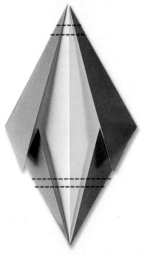

1 Make the Basic Form VIII but do it a little differently, so the edges aren't all lying right along the middle line. Then, following the dashed line, make an inside crimp fold to form the beak.

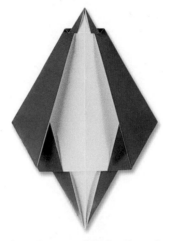

2 Then, make mountain fold followed by a valley fold, to create an accordion, right under the tip of the wing.

3 Fold the figure together in the middle. On the dashed line, form the head with a reverse fold. Pull the point of the beak slightly lower. To form the feet, make a cut on the crease, at the lower point of the form, from the bottom up to the belly.

4 First, fold the two cut foot sections upward and then to the front, as shown, so that the soles of the feet will stand flat on the ground.

5 Completed Papa Penguin.

BABY PENGUIN

1 Make Basic Form I, the Kite Fold, in a way so the edges don't lie exactly along the middle line.

2 Open the figure and fold the right and left corners to the inside.

3 Close the figure and, at the point, make a mountain fold and then a valley fold for the beak.

4 Fold the figure together in the middle and along the dashed lines. Form the head with a reverse fold, and the tail with a sink fold.

5 Along the dashed line fold the stomach on both sides of the figure with two sink folds, extending a little to the inside.

6 For a rounder baby's beak, you may fold the point of the beak slightly toward the inside. Finally, pull the end of the beak downward a little bit. Completed Baby Penguin.

REINDEER PART 1

1 Start with Basic Form VII. Inside reverse folds.

2 Valley fold both sides.

3 Valley fold in half. Rotate form.

4 Outside reverse fold.

5 Outside reverse folds.

6 Make cuts as shown.

7 Pleat folds.

8 Outside reverse fold.

9 Pleat fold both sides.

10 Tuck ears in.

11 Pleat folds.

12 Pull and crimp fold.

13 Inside reverse folds.

14 Mountain folds both sides.

15 Cuts and valley folds.

16 Completed part 1 (front) of Reindeer.

REINDEER PART II

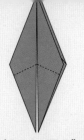

1 Start with Basic Form VII. Valley folds.

2 Turn over to other side.

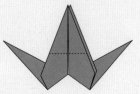

3 Valley fold.

4 Valley fold.

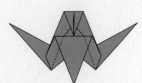

5 Valley folds.

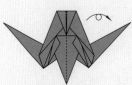

6 Fold in half, then rotate.

7 Outside reverse fold.

8 Inside reverse fold, both sides.

9 Inside reverse folds, both sides.

10 Completed part 2 (rear) of Reindeer.

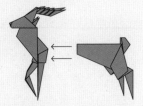

TO ATTACH Join both parts together, and apply glue to hold.

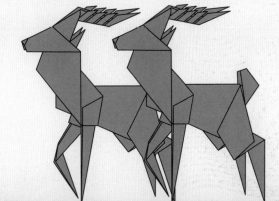

CRANE

1 Begin with Basic Form VI.

2 With opening at the top of the model, fold and unfold along dashed lines.

3 Open upper flap at the top point, pulling it down as far as possible. Press at left- and right-center corners so edges meet at the vertical midline. This will form a diamond.

4 Turn the model over. Repeat Steps 2–3.

5 Rotate model so opening is at the bottom. Fold left- and right-upper corners to vertical midline. Turn model over and repeat.

6 Unfold model to Basic Form VI. Fold the right-upper layer to the left side and the left-lower layer to the right side.

7 Repeat Steps 2–5.

8 Fold the right-upper layer to the left side and the left-lower layer to the right side.

9 Fold bottom-upper point up to the top point. Turn model over and repeat.

10 Fold the right-upper layer to the left side and the left-lower layer to the right side.

11 Pull "tail" point outward and press to fold in place.

12 Pull "neck" point outward and press to fold in place.

13 Crease neck along dashed line.

14 Reverse-fold by opening the neck and collapsing the tip to the inside.

15 Pull the wings in opposite directions until the "back" begins to flatten somewhat.

16 Completed Crane.

FLAPPING CRANE

1 Begin with a Basic Form VII.

2 Rotate model so opening is at the bottom. Crease along the dashed line and reverse-fold by opening flap and collapsing the tip to the inside.

3 Crease along the dashed line and reverse-fold remaining flap by opening it and collapsing the tip to the inside.

4 Crease neck along dashed line.

5 Reverse fold by opening the neck and collapsing the tip to the inside.

6 Fold wing down along dashed line. Turn model over and repeat.

7 Completed Flapping Crane.

8 To flap the Crane's wings, hold the base of its neck with one hand and pull on its tail with the other hand.

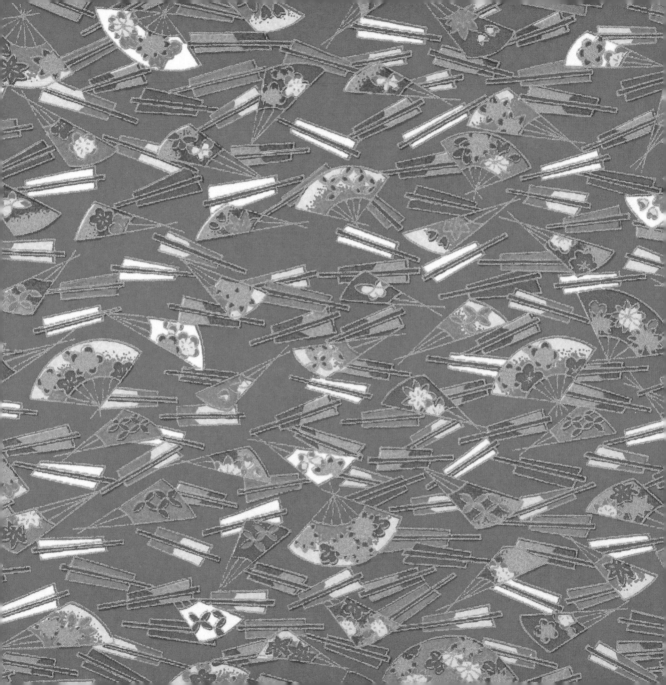

TURTLE

1 Start with a square paper, with the wrong side facing up. Fold the paper on the diagonal middle lines. Unfold.

2 Fold the four corners into the middle. Unfold.

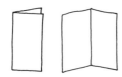

3 Fold paper vertically in the middle. The opposite edges must lie exactly one on top of the other. Open the fold.

4 Fold both sides towards the middle line. Open folds.

5 Repeat Step 3 in a horizontal direction. Open folds. The crease lines will cross each other in the middle.

6 Pull the sides and the corners of the figure upward by placing the double triangles at each of the small corners of the diagonals on top of each other.

7 Fold the lower and the upper edges onto the horizontal middle lines so that both the right and left edges lie along the vertical middle line at the same time.

8 Turn the figure over. Fold a "sink point" by putting together the square in the middle of the figure.

9 Completed Step 8.

10 Fold half of all four wings upward; then fold the four wings back again.

11 Open the figure entirely and make a reverse fold on each edge along the preliminary fold of step 8. Again, close the figure using steps 1–8.

12 Push from underneath, as shown, on the center of the figure, so the shape folds up and outward. You should now have a kind of shell shape with four feet.

13 Open the figure on one side and pull this side out so that the paper can lie doubled along the middle line. The point that arises here becomes the head of the Turtle. Hold the head in this position, and close the shell of the Turtle. In that way, folds appear on both sides of the head and prevent the head from refolding. Press this fold firmly from the outside.

14 Fold down a small corner at the back of the shell. Open this preliminary fold and press the small "double-triangle" that appears inward, as a sink fold. Make small sink folds on both lateral corners of the Turtle's shell, too.

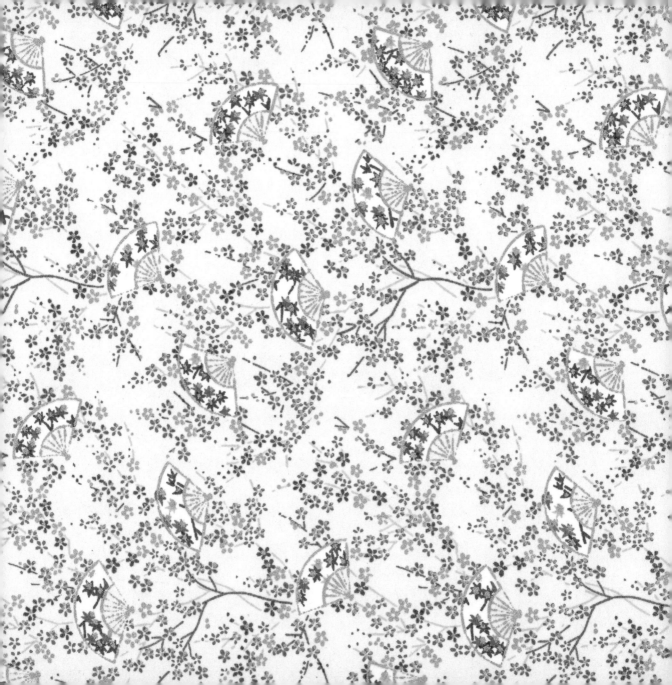

HORSESHOE CRAB

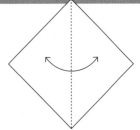

1 Start with square. Valley fold and unfold.

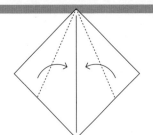

2 Fold both sides inward.

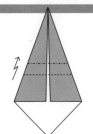

3 Pleat fold.

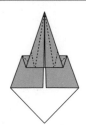

4 Squash folds.

5 Valley fold.

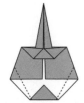

6 Valley folds.

7 Valley folds.

8 Turn over.

9 Valley fold.

10 Mountain fold in half.

11 Rotate.

12 Crimp fold.

13 Mountain folds both sides.

14 Valley fold and unfold.

15 Unfold to flatten.

16 Completed Horseshoe Crab.

SEAL

1 Basic Form VIII.

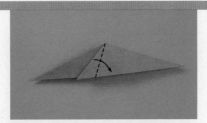

2 Fold model in half so opening is at the bottom.

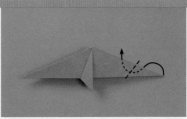

3 Fold upper flap to the center. Turn model over and repeat.

4 Crease along the dashed line and reverse fold by opening flap and collapsing the tip to the inside.

5 Crease along the dashed line and reverse fold remaining flap by opening it and collapsing the tip to the inside.

6 Crease neck and reverse fold by opening the neck and collapsing the tip to the inside.

7 Crease snout and reverse fold by opening and collapsing the tip to the inside.

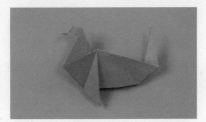

8 Crease nose and reverse fold by opening and collapsing the tip to the outside.

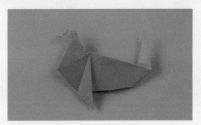

9 Completed Seal.

DOLPHIN PART 1

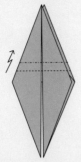

1 Start with Basic Form VII. Pleat fold through all layers.

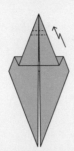

2 Repeat pleat fold through layers.

3 Make cuts as shown (to top layer only).

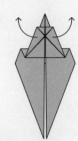

4 Valley folds.

5 Valley fold in half.

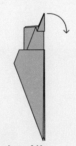

6 Pull and crimp fold.

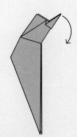

7 Pull and crimp fold.

8 Mountain fold.

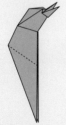

9 Valley folds.

10 Mountain fold both sides.

11 Cuts as shown.

12 Completed part 1 of Dolphin.

DOLPHIN PART II

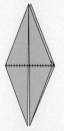

1 Start with Basic Form VII. Cut as shown.

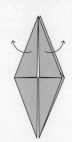

2 Valley folds.

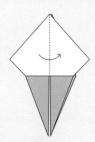

3 Valley fold in half.

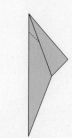

4 Outside reverse fold.

5 Mountain fold.

6 Pull paper outward at top; mountain fold below.

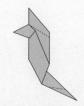

7 Outside reverse fold at top. Mountain fold below.

8 Valley fold and glue into position.

9 Completed part 2 of Dolphin.

TO ATTACH

1 Join both parts together as shown.

2 Valley fold both sides.

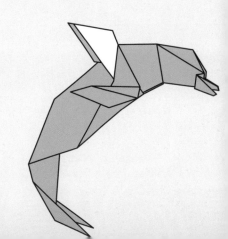

ANGELFISH

1 Trim paper to be rectangular (size variable). Valley fold paper in half.

2 Valley fold in direction of arrow.

3 Make cut as shown.

4 Unfold.

5 Unfold.

6 Valley fold in half.

7 Inside reverse folds.

8 Cuts to front layer only.

9 Valley fold cut parts.

10 Valley fold front and back.

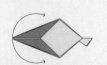

11 Inside reverse folds.

12 Valley fold front and back.

13 Mountain fold layer inward.

14 Valley fold layer and unfold.

15 Cut along crease. Valley fold.

16 Turn over to other side.

17 Mountain fold.

18 Cut as shown, valley fold.

19 Valley fold both side fins outward.

20 Turn over.

21 Add color.

22 Completed Angelfish.

CORAL FISH

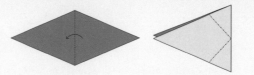

1 Valley fold in half.

2 Inside reverse folds.

3 Valley fold both front and back.

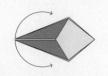

4 Inside reverse folds.

5 Valley fold both sides.

6 Outside reverse fold.

7 Repeat.

8 Valley fold both sides.

9 Outside reverse fold.

10 Repeat.

11 Valley fold layer to front.

12 Valley fold.

13 Mountain fold to inside.

14 Valley fold.

15 Mountain fold to inside.

16 Mountain fold to back.

17 Cut and valley fold out to sides both front and back.

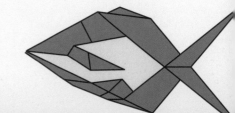

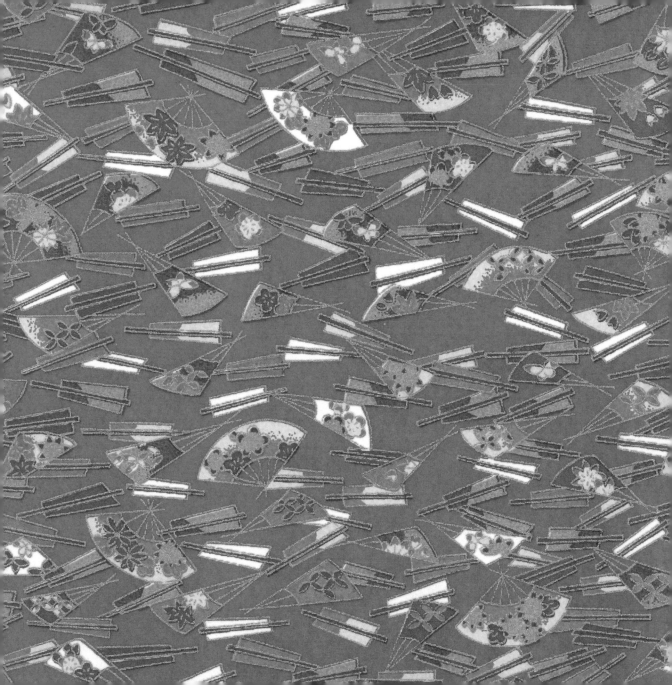

STINGRAY

1 Start with Basic Form VII. Valley folds.

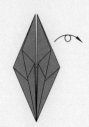

2 Turn over.

3 Squash fold.

4 Cut as shown. Valley folds.

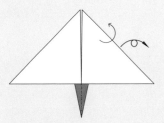

5 Mountain fold in half, then rotate into position of next step.

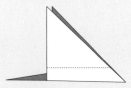

6 Valley fold both front and back.

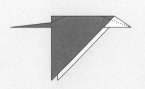

7 Valley folds to both sides.

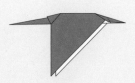

8 Valley fold both front and back.

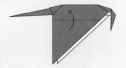

9 Valley and mountain folds.

10 Mountain fold both sides. Apply glue to center of form.

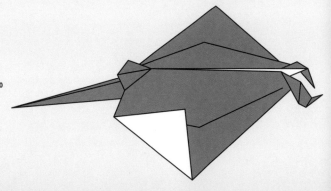

FLYING
FISH

1 Start with Basic Form VII. Valley folds.

2 Inside reverse folds.

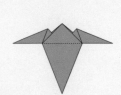

3 Valley folds.

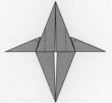

4 Valley folds. Squash at same time.

5 Valley folds.

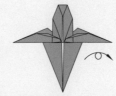

6 Turn over to other side.

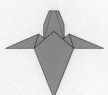

7 Valley folds.

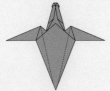

8 Valley folds.

9 Cut as shown.

10 Mountain fold in half, then rotate.

11 Mountain fold.

12 Valley fold.

13 Valley folds.

14 Open and flatten.

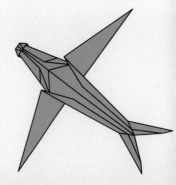

SWORDFISH PART I

1 Start with Basic Form VIII, then mountain fold in half.

2 Valley folds front and back.

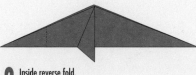

3 Inside reverse fold.

4 Valley folds front and back.

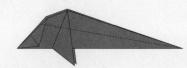

5 Valley folds front and back.

6 Valley folds, for "eyes."

7 Completed part 1 (rear) of Swordfish.

SWORDFISH PART II

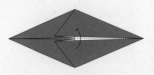

1 Start with Basic Form VIII, then valley fold in half.

2 Make cut through layers as indicated.

3 Valley folds to each side.

4 Mountain fold inward, both front and back.

5 Completed part 2 (front) of Swordfish.

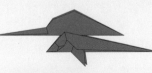

TO ATTACH

1 Attach parts 1 and 2 together as shown; lightly glue to hold.

2 Make "top fin" cuts both sides as shown. Lightly, inside reverse fold top "tail fin."

3 In same way, outside reverse fold lower "tail fin." Squash fold both "side fins."

4 Completed Swordfish.

KILLER WHALE PART I

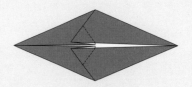

1 Start with Basic Form VIII, then valley folds.

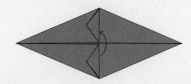

2 Valley fold in half.

3 Inside reverse fold, as shown.

4 Valley folds front and back.

5 Valley folds front and back.

6 Valley folds front and back for "eyes."

7 Completed part I (top) of Killer Whale.

KILLER WHALE PART II

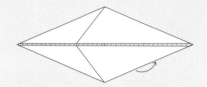

1 Start with Basic Form VIII, then mountain fold in half.

2 Valley fold both sides.

3 Inside reverse fold.

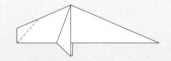

4 Mountain fold front and back.

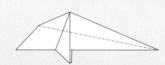

5 Mountain fold front and back.

6 Completed part 2 (bottom) of Killer Whale.

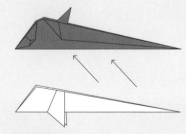

TO ATTACH

1 Put parts 1 and 2 together, as shown, and glue front body part to hold.

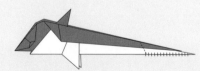

2 Cut through layers as indicated, lightly valley fold "tail fin" layers front and back to separate.

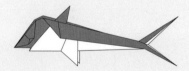

3 Completed Killer Whale.

FLYING FOX

1 Start with Basic Form VII; pull open in direction of arrows.

2 Squash fold as shown.

3 Cut, then unfold.

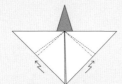

4 Pleat folds on both sides.

5 Squash folds.

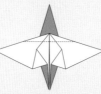

6 Valley folds.

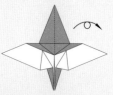

7 Valley fold in half, then rotate form.

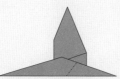

8 Inside reverse folds.

9 Inside reverse folds front and back.

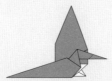

10 Again, inside reverse folds.

11 Now outside reverse folds.

12 Valley folds front and back.

13 Outside reverse fold.

14 Pleat fold.

15 Inside reverse fold.

16 Make cuts as shown, then valley folds for "ears."

17 Squash fold "ears" to open.

18 Valley fold "wings" front and back.

19 Completed Flying Fox.

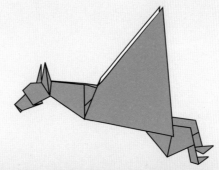

PELYCOSAUR PART I

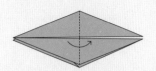

1 Start with Basic Form VII, then valley fold.

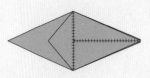

2 Cut only the front.

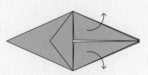

3 Valley fold open the cut parts.

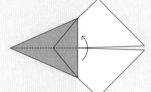

4 Valley fold in half.

5 Pleat fold.

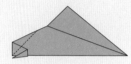

6 Valley fold both sides.

7 Valley fold both sides.

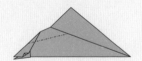

8 Mountain fold front and back.

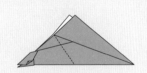

9 Valley fold both sides.

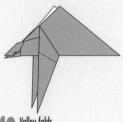

10 Valley folds.

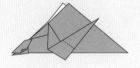

11 Valley folds.

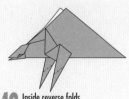

12 Inside reverse folds.

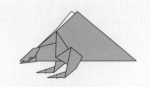

13 Outside reverse folds.

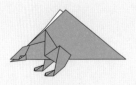

14 Completed part 1 (front) of Pelycosaur.

PELYCOSAUR PART II

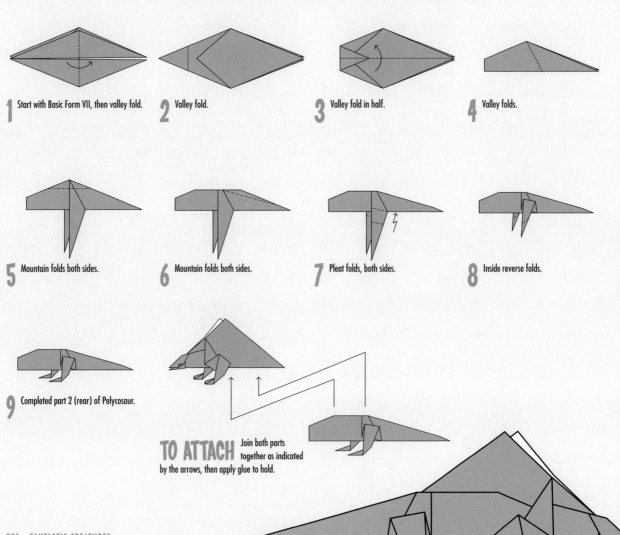

1 Start with Basic Form VII, then valley fold.

2 Valley fold.

3 Valley fold in half.

4 Valley folds.

5 Mountain folds both sides.

6 Mountain folds both sides.

7 Pleat folds, both sides.

8 Inside reverse folds.

9 Completed part 2 (rear) of Pelycosaur.

TO ATTACH Join both parts together as indicated by the arrows, then apply glue to hold.

VELOCIRAPTOR PART I

1 Start with Basic Form VII, then valley fold.

2 Cut as shown.

3 Valley fold.

4 Pleat fold both flaps together, and rotate.

5 Valley fold in half.

6 Inside reverse fold.

7 Inside reverse fold.

8 Pull in direction of arrow, and squash fold.

9 Valley fold front and back.

10 Outside reverse fold.

11 Inside reverse fold.

12 Make cuts to both front and back.

13 Mountain folds.

14 Inside reverse fold.

15 Valley fold front and back.

16 Inside reverse fold.

17 Inside reverse fold.

18 Inside reverse fold.

19 Outside reverse fold.

20 Turn over to the other side.

21 Repeat steps 14–19 on this side.

22 Completed part 1 (front) of Velociraptor.

VELOCIRAPTOR PART II

1 Start with Basic Form VII. Valley fold.

2 Squash folds.

3 Valley fold.

4 Valley folds.

5 Valley folds.

6 Valley fold.

7 Valley folds.

8 Valley folds.

9 Fold in half.

10 Rotate.

11 Valley fold front and back.

12 Inside reverse fold front and back.

13 Inside reverse fold front and back.

14 Inside reverse fold.

15 Outside reverse fold.

16 Completed part 2 (rear) of Velociraptor.

TO ATTACH Join both parts together as indicated by the arrows, then apply glue to hold.

TYRANNOSAUR PART I

1 Start with Basic Form VII. Inside reverse folds, and rotate.

2 Valley fold.

3 Cut, then valley fold.

4 Valley folds.

5 Pleat folds.

6 Valley fold in half.

7 Inside reverse fold.

8 Outside reverse fold.

9 Pull up and squash fold.

10 Outside reverse fold.

11 Inside reverse fold.

12 Pull up and squash fold.

13 Inside reverse folds.

14 Outside reverse folds.

15 Completed part 1 (front) of Tyrannosaur.

TYRANNOSAUR PART II

1 Start with Basic Form VII. Valley fold.

2 Valley fold in half.

3 Valley fold front and back.

4 Inside reverse fold front and back, then rotate.

5 Inside reverse fold front and back.

6 Inside reverse fold.

7 Outside reverse fold.

8 Mountain fold front and back.

9 Completed part 2 (rear) of Tyrannosaur.

TO ATTACH
Join both parts together as indicated and apply glue to hold. When dry, you can bend dinosaur into a lifelike pose for display.

STEGOSAUR PART I

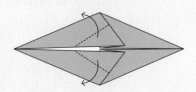

1 Start with Basic Form VIII. Make valley folds and squash folds (see next diagram).

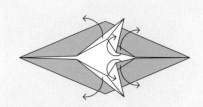

2 Appearance just before completion.

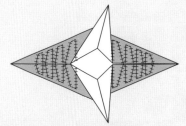

3 Make cuts as shown, then valley fold out.

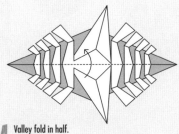

4 Valley fold in half.

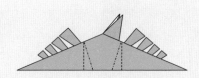

5 Pleat folds.

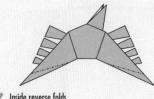

6 Inside reverse folds.

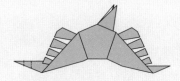

7 Pleat fold, forming "mouth."

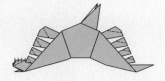

8 Cut and pleat fold both sides of "head," mountain fold down "body" as shown.

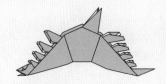

9 Completed part 1 (head and back) of Stegosaur.

STEGOSAUR PART II

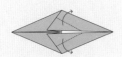

1 Start with Basic Form VIII. Make valley folds, then squash.

2 Appearance just before completion.

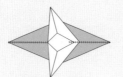

3 Make cuts as shown.

4 Valley fold in half.

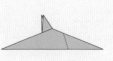

5 Valley fold both front and back.

6 Mountain fold both sides.

7 Inside reverse fold both front and back.

8 Valley fold.

9 Mountain fold.

10 Outside reverse fold.

11 Turn over to the other side.

12 Valley fold.

13 Mountain fold.

14 Outside reverse fold.

15 Completed part 2 (body) of Stegosaur.

TO ATTACH Lower part 1 into center of part 2 as shown, and apply glue to hold.

PARASAUROLOPHUS PART 1

1 Start with Basic Form VII. Valley fold both sides.

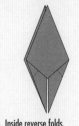

2 Inside reverse folds.

3 Valley folds.

4 Make cut as shown, then valley fold in half.

5 Rotate.

6 Inside reverse fold both sides.

7 Inside reverse fold both sides.

8 Inside reverse folds.

9 Inside reverse fold.

10 Inside reverse (hidden) for good angle.

11 Inside reverse fold.

12 Valley fold.

13 Valley fold.

14 Valley fold.

15 Valley fold.

16 Outside reverse fold.

17 Outside reverse fold.

18 Mountain fold both sides.

19 Mountain fold both sides.

20 Completed part 1 (front) of Parasaurolophus.

PARASAUROLOPHUS PART II

1 Start with Basic Form VII. Valley folds.

2 Turn over to the other side.

3 Valley fold.

4 Valley fold.

5 Fold in half, then rotate.

6 Inside reverse fold.

7 Pleat fold.

8 Inside reverse fold.

9 Inside reverse fold upper leg, mountain fold tail.

10 Turn over.

11 Inside reverse fold.

12 Pleat fold.

13 Inside reverse fold upper leg and mountain fold tail. Inside reverse fold foot.

14 Completed part 2 (rear) of Parasaurolophus.

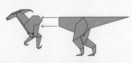

TO ATTACH Join both parts together as indicated by the arrows, then apply glue to hold.

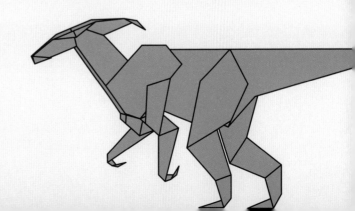

PACHYCEPHALOSAUR PART I

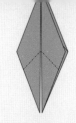

1 Start with Basic Form VII. Inside reverse folds.

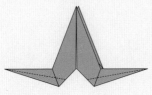

2 Valley folds.

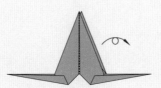

3 Valley fold in half. Rotate form.

4 Inside reverse fold.

5 Inside reverse fold.

6 Inside reverse fold.

7 Partial inside reverse fold, crimping upwards.

8 Outside reverse fold.

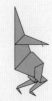

9 Inside reverse fold.

10 Outside reverse fold.

11 Mountain fold.

12 Outside reverse fold, then outside reverse again.

13 Completed part 1 (front) of Pachycephalosaur.

PACHYCEPHALOSAUR PART II

1 Start with Basic Form VII. Valley fold.

2 Valley fold in half and rotate.

3 Valley fold front and back.

4 Rotate.

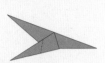

5 Inside reverse fold.

6 Inside reverse fold.

7 Inside reverse fold.

8 Outside reverse fold.

9 Inside reverse fold leg, then mountain fold tail.

10 Turn over to other side.

11 Valley fold.

12 Inside reverse fold.

13 Inside reverse folds.

14 Inside reverse fold upper leg, then mountain fold tail.

15 Outside reverse fold.

16 Completed part 2 (rear) of Pachycephalosaur.

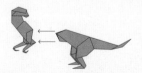
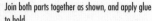

TO ATTACH Join both parts together as shown, and apply glue to hold.

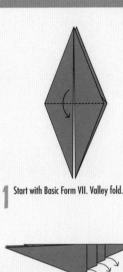

1 Start with Basic Form VII. Valley fold.

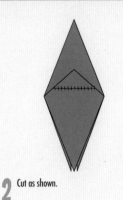

2 Cut as shown.

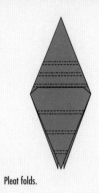

3 Pleat folds.

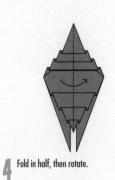

4 Fold in half, then rotate.

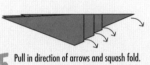

5 Pull in direction of arrows and squash fold.

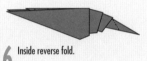

6 Inside reverse fold.

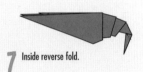

7 Inside reverse fold.

8 Pleat fold.

9 Mountain fold front and back.

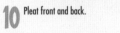

10 Pleat front and back.

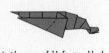

11 Inside reverse folds front and back.

12 Inside reverse folds front and back.

13 Pull and squash fold to shape.

14 Outside reverse folds.

15 Outside reverse folds.

16 Completed part 1 (front) of Ankylosaur.

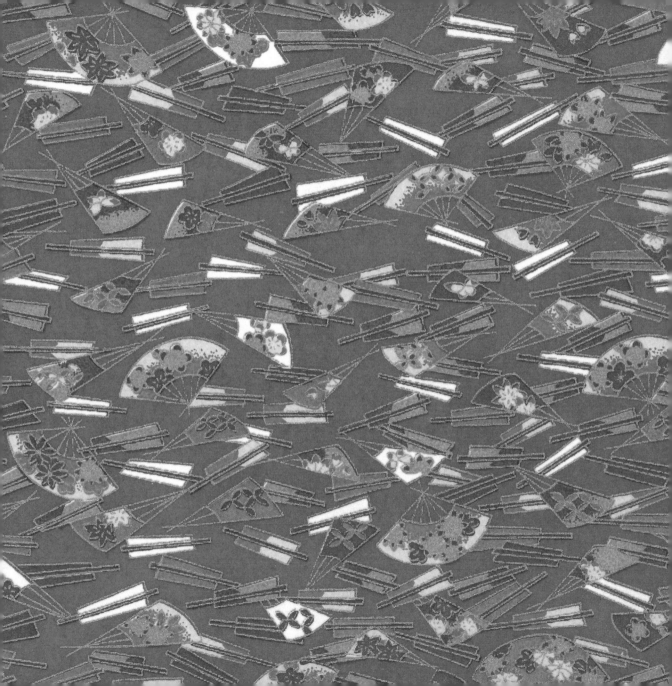

ANKYLOSAUR PART II

1 Start with Basic Form VII. Valley fold.

2 Cut as shown.

3 Cut as shown.

4 Valley fold in half, then rotate.

5 Valley fold front and back.

6 Pull in direction of arrow, and squash fold.

7 Mountain folds front and back.

8 Outside reverse fold.

9 Pleat folds.

10 Inside reverse fold.

11 Pull in direction of arrows and squash fold.

12 Valley fold front and back.

13 Inside reverse fold.

14 Mountain fold.

15 Mountain fold.

16 Outside reverse fold.

17 Turn over to the other side.

18 Inside reverse fold, then repeat steps 12–17.

19 Outside reverse fold.

20 Complete part 2 (rear) of Ankylosaur.

TO ATTACH Join both parts together as indicated by the arrows and apply glue to hold.

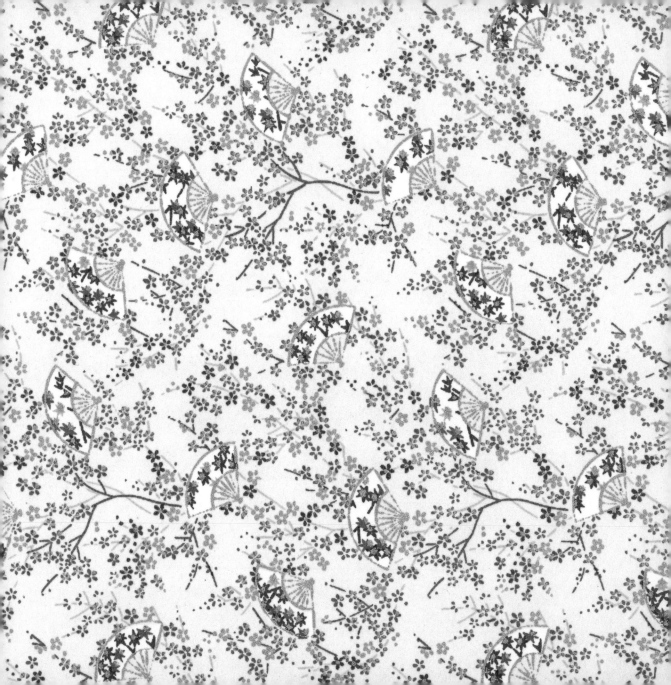

DILOPHOSAUR PART I

1 Start with Basic Form VII. Inside reverse folds.

2 Mountain folds.

3 Valley folds, then turn over to other side.

4 Valley fold left and right toward center.

5 Valley fold left and right side. Valley fold in half then rotate.

6 Inside reverse fold.

7 Inside reverse folds.

8 Valley fold.

9 Cut as shown, then valley fold cut parts. Inside reverse fold legs.

10 Cut as shown.

11 Valley fold.

12 Mountain fold both sides.

13 Inside reverse fold.

14 Pull down on flaps to loosen folds, then valley fold in the direction of arrows.

15 Outside reverse fold.

16 Pleat fold.

17 Outside reverse fold.

18 Now mountain fold.

19 Inside reverse folds.

20 Outside reverse folds.

21 Pull frill into position, as shown.

22 Completed part 1 (front) of Dilophosaur.

DILOPHOSAUR PART II

1 Start with Basic Form VII. Valley fold.

2 Turn over.

3 Valley fold.

4 Mountain fold in half, then rotate.

5 Inside reverse folds front and back.

6 Mountain fold both front and back.

7 Outside reverse fold both sides.

8 Inside reverse fold.

9 Outside reverse folds.

10 Completed part 2 (rear) of Dilophosaur.

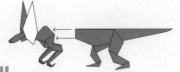

TO ATTACH
Join both parts together as shown, and apply glue to hold.

TABLE

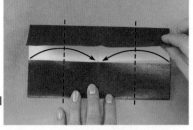

1 Begin with a square. Fold in half in both directions (wrong side of paper is inside). Unfold to show creases. Fold top and bottom edges to the horizontal midline (wrong side of paper is inside).

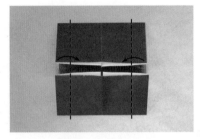

2 Rotate model. Fold new top and bottom edges to horizontal midline, as in Step 1.

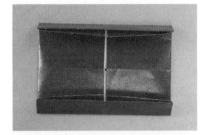

3 Rotate model. Fold top and bottom edges one third of the distance to the horizontal midline. Unfold last two folds. Fold each corner to meet creases.

4 Unfold the corners. Place your index finger between layers at the bottom right corner as indicated and press to flatten. Repeat for each corner.

5 Rotate model.

6 Fold two side flaps upward.

7 Turn model over so table stands. Completed Table.

CHAIR SET, CHAIR A

1 Begin with Basic Form III.

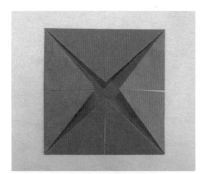

2 Turn model over. Fold each corner to center.

3 Turn model over. Fold each corner to center.

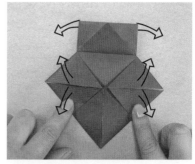

4 Turn model over. Push bottom-upper point of one diamond to top of model and pull inside edges to outside. Press to flatten.

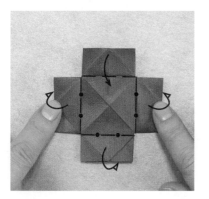

5 Rotate model and repeat previous action for each side.

6 Fold one side forward and three sides backward so model will stand. Completed Chair A.

TIP: INSERT A FOLDED PIECE OF PAPER INTO THE TOP EDGE OF THE CHAIR BACK TO COVER THE GAP.

CHAIR SET, CHAIR B

1 Begin with Basic Form III.

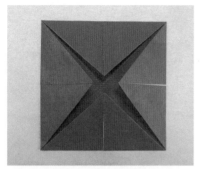

2 Turn model over. Fold each corner to center.

3 Turn model over. Fold each corner to center.

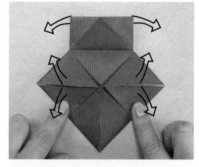

4 Turn model over. Push bottom-upper point of one diamond to top of model and pull inside edges to outside. Press to flatten.

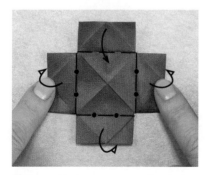

5 Rotate model and repeat previous action for each side.

6 Fold one side forward and three sides backward so model will stand. Completed Chair B. Place with Chair A around Table.

TIP: INSERT A FOLDED PIECE OF PAPER INTO THE TOP EDGE OF THE CHAIR BACK TO COVER THE GAP.

SAILBOAT

1 Begin with Basic Form III.

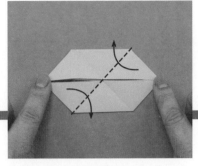

2 Refer to Basic Form IV. Fold Basic Form III as if it were a simple square to produce Basic Form IV.

3 Lift each flap slightly. Hold the top-right flap with your right-hand thumb and index finger. Hold the bottom-left flap with your left-hand thumb and index finger. Fold top-right flap over and to the right so it is against the body of the model.

4 Fold top-right flap and body of the model as one diagonally to the back so that the point meets the point of the bottom-left flap.

5 Rotate so these two flaps make up the bottom edge of the model.

6 Completed Sailboat.

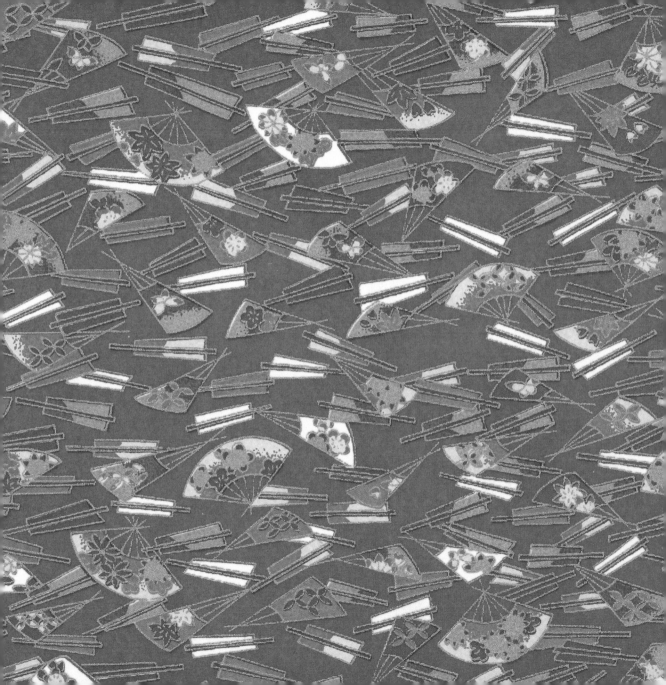

PAPER HEART

1 Begin with a square. Fold in half (wrong side of the paper is inside).

2 Unfold. Rotate and fold in half in other direction (wrong side of paper is inside).

3 Unfold. Fold bottom edge to the horizontal midline (wrong side of paper is inside).

4 Turn model over. Fold bottom-left corner to vertical midline.

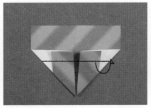

5 Fold bottom-right corner to vertical midline.

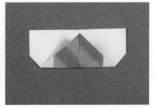

6 Turn model over. Fold bottom corner to top edge.

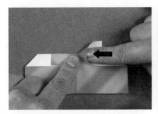

7 Turn model over. Rotate and place your index finger between layers on the right side as indicated.

8 Press to flatten.

9 Repeat Steps 7–8 for left side.

10 Turn model over. Fold top-left corner of heart to back.

11 Repeat Step 10 for top-right corner of heart.

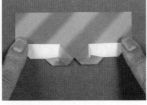

12 Turn model over. Fold each corner on heart along the dashed lines.

13 Turn model over. Fold each side to the back along the dashed lines.

14 Completed Paper Heart.

SLEIGH PART I

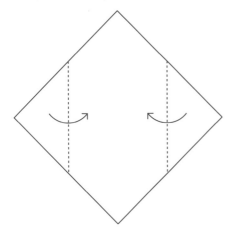

1 Make valley folds to center.

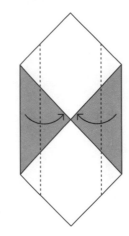

2 Again, valley folds to center.

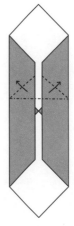

3 Valley/mountain folds to boxlike shape; glue to hold.

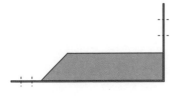

4 Side view, mountain folds.

5 Completed part 1 (top) of Sleigh.

SLEIGH PART II

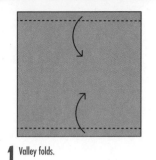

1 Valley folds.

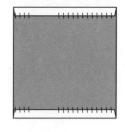

2 Make cuts as shown.

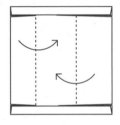

3 Valley folds, right side then left.

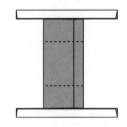

4 Valley folds.

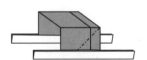

5 Mountain folds both sides.

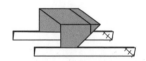

6 Make cuts as shown, and discard.

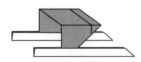

7 Completed part 2 (runners) of Sleigh.

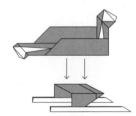

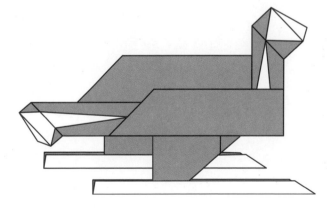

TO ATTACH Join Sleigh parts 1 and 2 together as shown and apply glue to hold.

GREMLIN MASK

1 Start with half-square triangle. Valley fold.

2 Valley folds.

3 Valley folds.

4 Mountain fold.

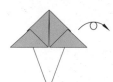

5 Rotate.

6 Valley folds.

7 Close-up.

8 Valley folds, unfold.

9 Valley folds, unfold.

10 Pinch together at corners, and valley fold inward.

11 Back to full view.

12 Pleat fold.

13 Valley fold.

14 Mountain fold.

15 Valley folds.

16 Valley fold tip.

17 Valley folds and squash folds.

18 Mountain fold in half.

19 Pull and crimp fold.

20 Open out folds.

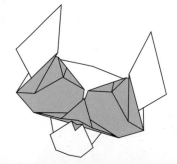

COWBOY HAT

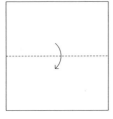

1 Start with square sheet; valley fold.

2 Squash fold.

3 Turn to other side.

4 Squash fold.

5 Valley fold to crease.

6 Valley fold to crease.

7 Undo folds.

8 Pleat fold.

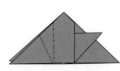

9 Repeat steps 5–8 on opposite end.

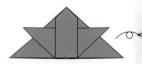

10 Turn to other side.

11 Repeat same steps, 5–8, on each end this side.

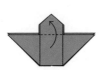

12 Valley fold, both sides.

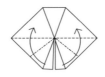

13 Pleat fold sides, front and back, squashing underfolds.

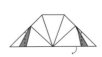

14 Unfold, then valley, bringing corners together, and glue.

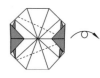

15 Valley folds to add shape to "brim." Rotate.

16 View of shaped "hat." Rotate to front.

17 Open out, loosen folds as shown.

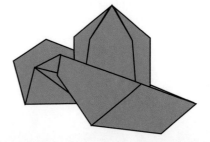

JACK-O'-LANTERN

1 Valley fold then unfold.

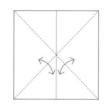

2 Valley folds then unfold, to crease.

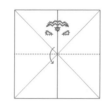

3 Make cuts (for face), then valley fold.

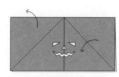

4 Mountain fold and valley fold.

5 Unfold.

6 Squash fold.

7 Repeat squash fold on back layer.

8 This is Basic Form V; now, valley folds.

9 Valley folds.

10 Turn over.

11 Valley folds. Look closer, now, at next steps.

12 Valley fold, front and back.

13 Valley fold, front and back.

14 Valley and unfold front and back, then tuck flaps into pockets as shown.

15 Push top down and pull open sides at same time.

16 Appearance before completion.

17 Completed Jack-O'-Lanterns.

CRAYON

1 Trim origami paper into a 7 1/2" x 3 1/4" (19 x 8 cm) rectangle. Set aside the remaining paper strip.

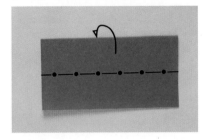

2 Fold paper in half (pink side of paper is inside).

3 Unfold and fold left edge 1/2" (1.3 cm) to the right.

4 Turn model over. Fold top- and bottom-left corners to the horizontal midline.

5 Fold top- and bottom-left corners again to the horizontal midline.

6 Turn model over. Fold left edge to the right.

7 Turn model over. Fold top and bottom edges to meet at the horizontal midline.

8 Turn model over. Rotate and adjust side edges so the shaft of the crayon is slightly larger than the slope on its tip.

9 Completed Crayon. For decoration, from the remaining paper, fashion a stripe and glue it onto the crayon.

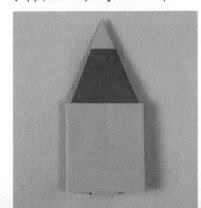

PAPER CUP

1 Begin with a square. Fold in half diagonally. Crease along dashed line.

2 Fold right corner to meet opposite point of crease.

3 Crease top-upper corner along dashed line.

4 Fold left corner to meet opposite point.

5 Tuck top-upper corner into top triangle.

NOTE The model will look like this after making the tuck.

6 Turn model over. Rotate and fold top corner toward center.

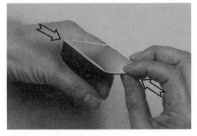

7 Open model by pushing in on both sides.

8 Completed Paper Cup.

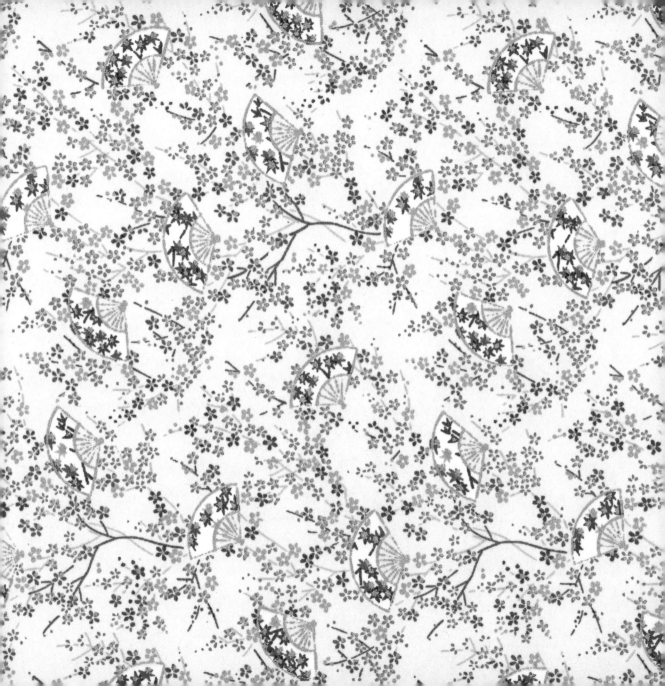

SNACK CUP

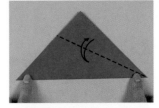

1 Begin with a square. Fold in half diagonally. Crease along dashed line.

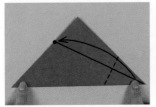

2 Fold right corner to meet opposite point of crease.

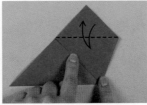

3 Crease top-upper corner along dashed line.

4 Fold left corner to meet opposite point.

5 Tuck top-upper corner into top triangle.

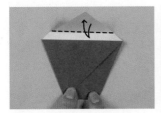

6 Crease top corner along dashed line.

7 Tuck top corner inside cup.

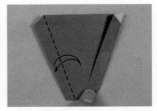

8 Turn model over. Crease left and right sides along the dashed lines.

9 Turn model over.

10 Crease the bottom along the dashed line.

11 Open model by flattening left, right, and bottom sides from the inside.

12 Pinch each bottom corner and fold toward the center for a flat bottom.

13 Completed Snack Cup.

CUP HOLDER PART I

1 Begin with a square. Fold in half (right side of the paper is inside).

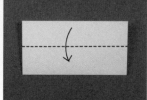

2 Fold top-upper edge along dashed line to fold.

NOTE The model will look like this after making the fold.

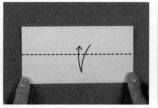

3 Turn model over. Crease along dashed line.

4 Fold all corners along dashed lines to horizontal midline.

NOTE For ease in working, rotate the model and make the folds at one end; then repeat for remaining end.

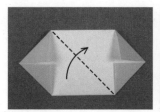

5 Fold left side up and to the right along dashed line.

NOTE The model will look like this after making the fold.

6 Unfold last fold. Fold right side up and to the left along the dashed line.

NOTE The model will look like this after making the fold.

7 Unfold the last fold to show the creases.

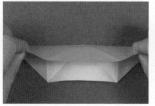

8 Fold model in half along horizontal midline (wrong side is inside).

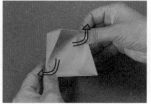

9 Turn the model upright. Insert your thumbs between the layers and pull edges outward, turning the model inside out and creating a flat bottom.

10 Completed Part I of Cup Holder.

CUP HOLDER PART II

1 Begin with a square. Fold in half (right side of the paper is inside).

2 Fold top-upper edge along dashed line to fold.

NOTE The model will look like this after making the fold.

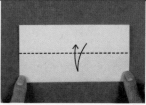

3 Turn model over. Crease along dashed line.

4 Fold all corners along dashed lines to horizontal midline.

NOTE For ease in working, rotate the model and make the folds at one end; then repeat for remaining end.

5 Fold left side up and to the right along dashed line.

NOTE The model will look like this after making the fold.

6 Unfold last fold. Fold right side up and to the left along the dashed line.

NOTE The model will look like this after making the fold.

7 Unfold the last fold to show the creases.

8 Fold model in half along horizontal midline (wrong side is inside).

9 Turn the model upright. Insert your thumbs between the layers and pull edges outward, turning the model inside out and creating a flat bottom.

10 Completed Part II of Cup Holder.

TO ATTACH

Set one model within the other. Completed Cup Holder.

CANDY CUP

1 Begin with Basic Form III.

2 Fold Basic Form III as if it were a simple square to change the form and produce Basic Form VI.

3 Push bottom-upper point to top of model and press to flatten. Turn model over and repeat.

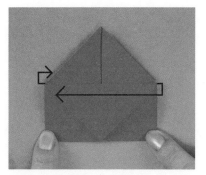

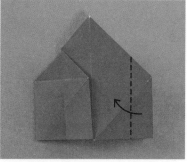

4 Rotate the model. Fold the right-upper layer to the left side and the left-lower layer to the right side.

NOTE The model will look like this after making the folds.

5 Fold each side edge to center along dashed lines. Turn model over and repeat.

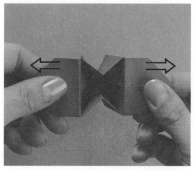

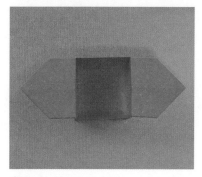

6 Fold top-upper corner down to bottom of model. Turn model over and repeat.

7 Open model by pulling the resulting flaps outward.

8 Completed Candy Cup.
The model is shown as viewed from the top.

UTENSIL HOLDER

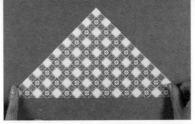

1 Start with square. Fold in half diagonally (wrong side of paper is inside).

2 Unfold. Fold in half diagonally in other direction (wrong side of paper is inside).

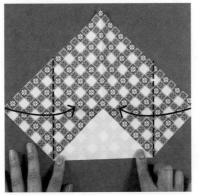

3 Unfold to show creases. Fold left, right, and bottom corners to center.

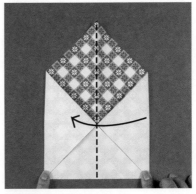

4 Fold model in half along dashed line.

5 Using a pair of decorative-edged scissors, trim along top angled edge.

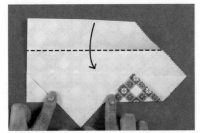

6 Unfold last fold. Turn model over and fold left and right sides to center along the dashed lines.

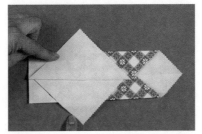

NOTE The model will look like this after making the folds. The left and right sides will be overlapping slightly.

7 Turn model over. Completed Utensil Holder.

SWAN BOX

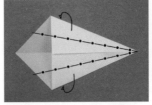

1 Begin with an Basic Form I: Kite Fold.

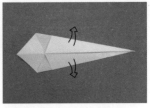

2 Turn model over. Fold top and bottom corners to horizontal midline.

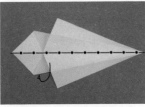

3 Pull flaps out from behind. Fold in half (to the back) along horizontal midline.

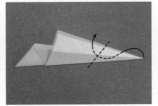

4 Crease along dashed line.

5 Reverse fold by opening the model and collapsing the tip to the inside, keeping the center fold at the center.

NOTE The model will look like this after making the folds.

6 Fold along dashed line.

7 Tuck corner under top wing.

8 Crease upper and lower flaps along dashed line.

9 Reverse fold by opening each flap and collapsing each tip to the inside.

10 Fold each wing downward so top edge meets bottom fold.

11 Crease neck along dashed line.

12 Reverse fold by opening the neck and collapsing the tip to the inside. Push the tail toward the inside of the model.

13 Completed Swan Box.

LETTER HOLDER

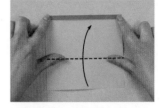

1 Begin with a square. Fold top edge 1" (2.5 cm) toward the center.

2 Fold bottom edge two-thirds of the distance toward top edge.

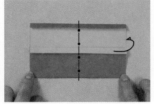

3 Fold top edge of upper flap 1" (2.5 cm) toward the bottom edge.

4 Turn model over. Fold left side to the right so model is folded in half.

5 Unfold last fold.

6 Rotate model. Fold left and right sides to vertical midline.

NOTE If you were to turn the model over, it would look like this after making the folds.

7 Place your index finger between layers on the left side and press to flatten.

8 Repeat Step 7 for the right side.

9 Fold and unfold left and right points along dashed lines.

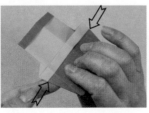

10 Reverse fold by pushing the previous fold on left and right toward inside of model.

11 Glue the flaps onto the back side of the model to secure.

12 Completed Letter Holder.

EASTER BASKET

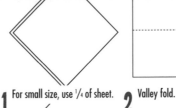

1 For small size, use ¼ of sheet.

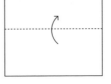

2 Valley fold.

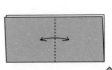

3 Valley fold, then unfold.

4 Inside reverse folds.

5 Inside reverse fold all four corners.

6 Valley fold both sides.

7 Valley folds.

8 Add strip of paper.

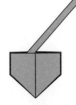

9 Valley folds.

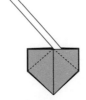

10 Turn over to other side.

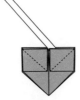

11 Valley folds.

12 Valley folds.

13 Insert strip as shown.

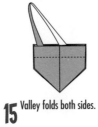

14 Valley folds.

15 Valley folds both sides.

16 Valley folds.

17 Valley folds.

18 Valley folds.

19 Mountain folds.

20 Repeat on all basket corners.

21 Pull to open out basket, mountain folding bottom to flatten.

CROW

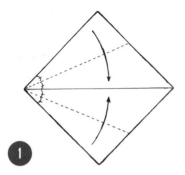

1

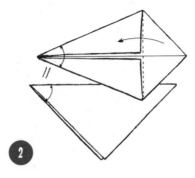

2

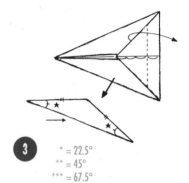

3

* = 22.5°
** = 45°
*** = 67.5°
Learn these geometry facts.

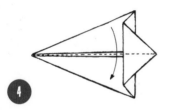

4

5

Inside reverse fold.

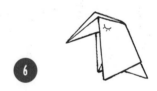

6

CAT

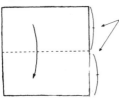

1

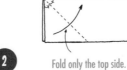

2 Fold only the top side.

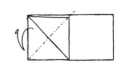

3

4

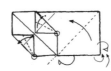

5 For a single-colored body, fold this part to the inside.

6

7

8

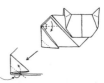

9 For stability, fold only the inner layers.

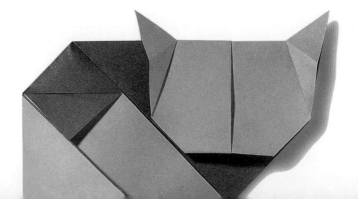

DRAGONFLY

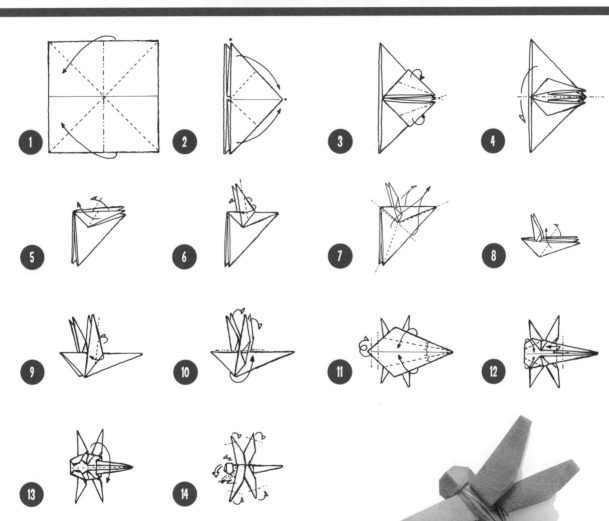

MOUSE

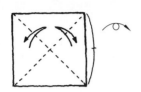

1

2

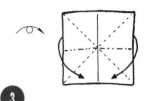

3

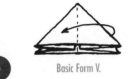

4

Basic Form V.

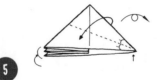

5

6

7

8

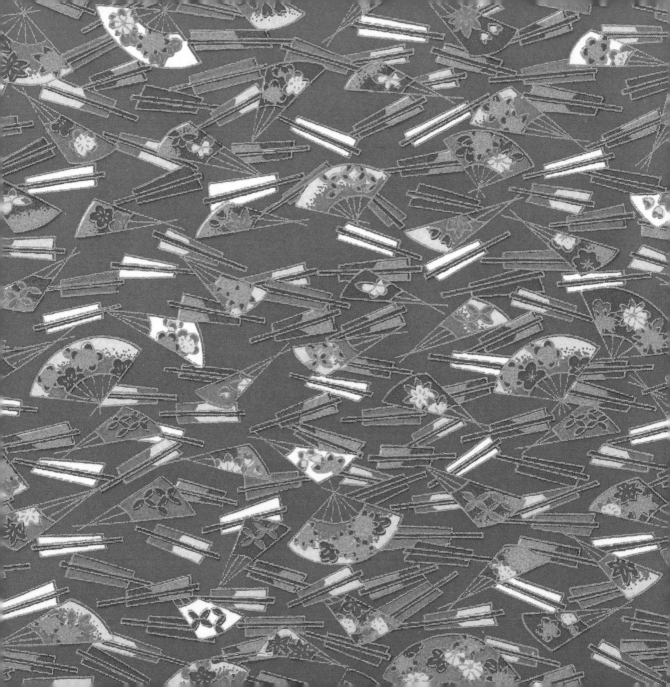

FLYING DOVE

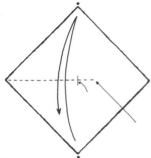

1 Fold somewhat beyond the center.

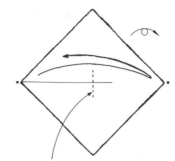

2 Fold only in the center area.

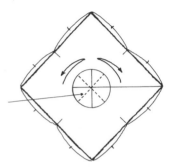

3 Fold only in the center area. Bring the right and left corners together.

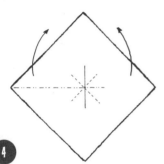

4

5

6 Reverse fold to the inside.

7 Fold out only the outer sides.

8 Reverse fold inwards for the head and beak.

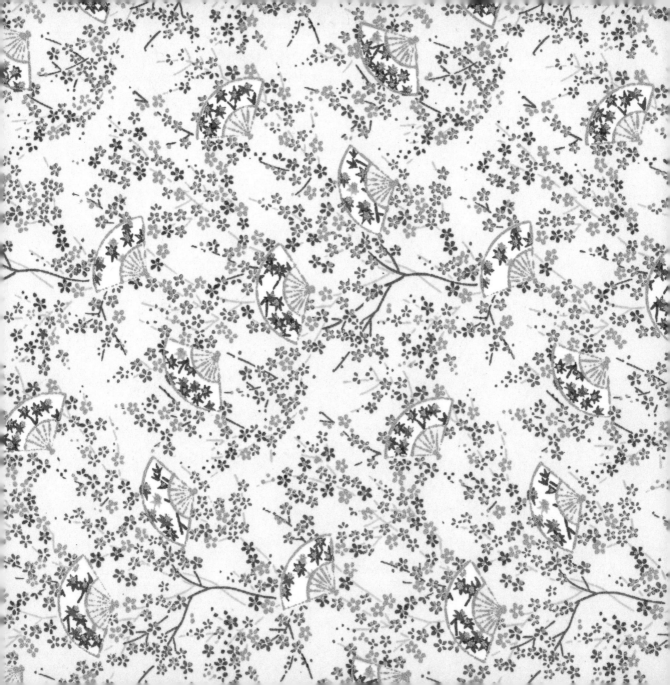

WHALE

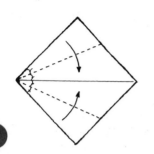

1

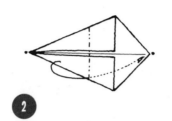

2

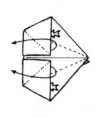

3

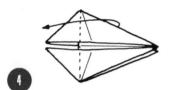

4

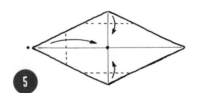

5

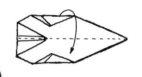

6

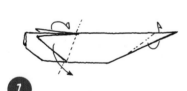

7

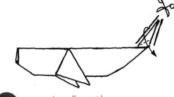

8

A small cut with
a big effect!

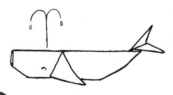

9

BEAR

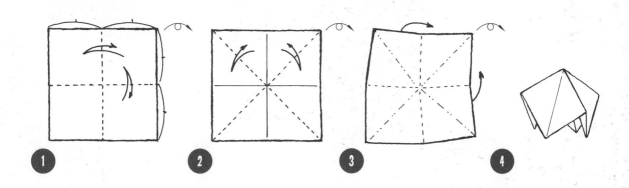

1 2 3 4

CRANE

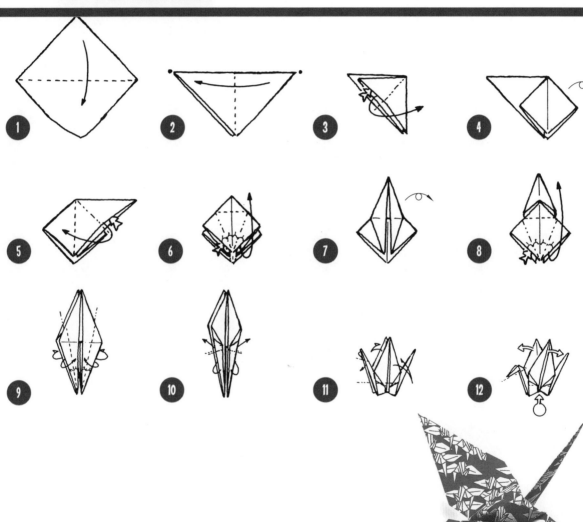

ORIZURU

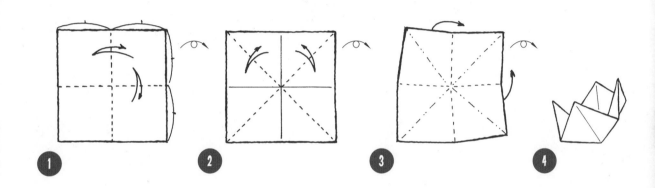

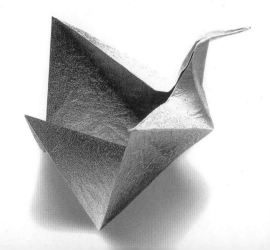

FISH MOUTH

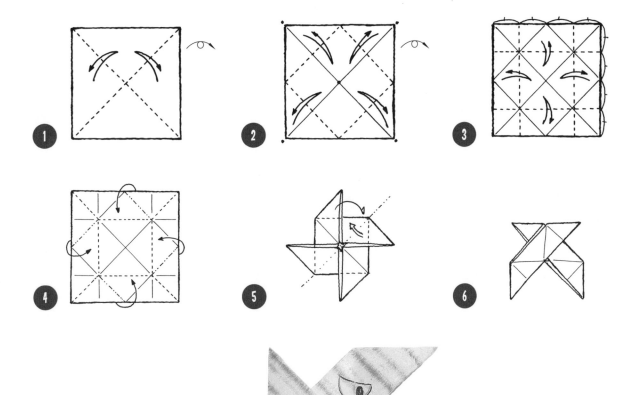

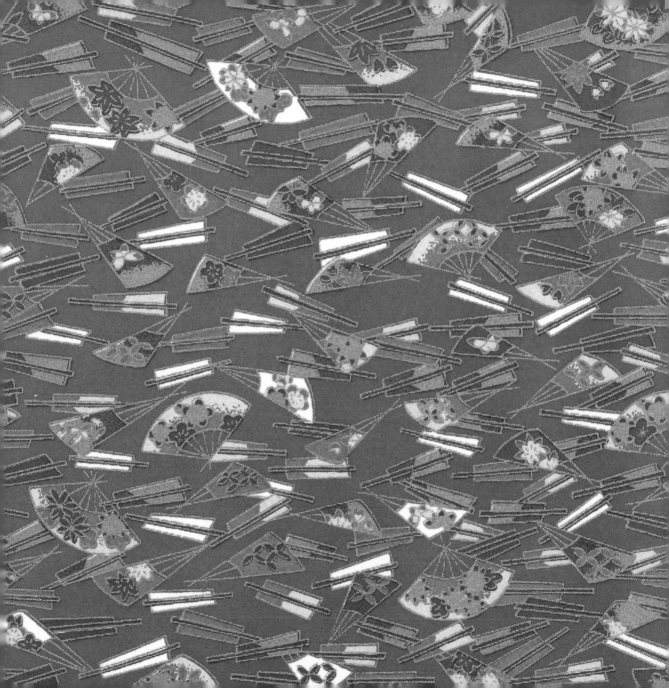

CAT'S FACE

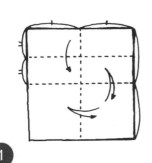

1

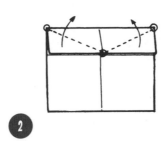

2

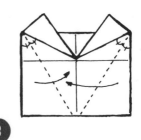

3

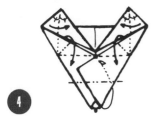

4

5

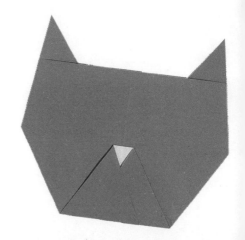

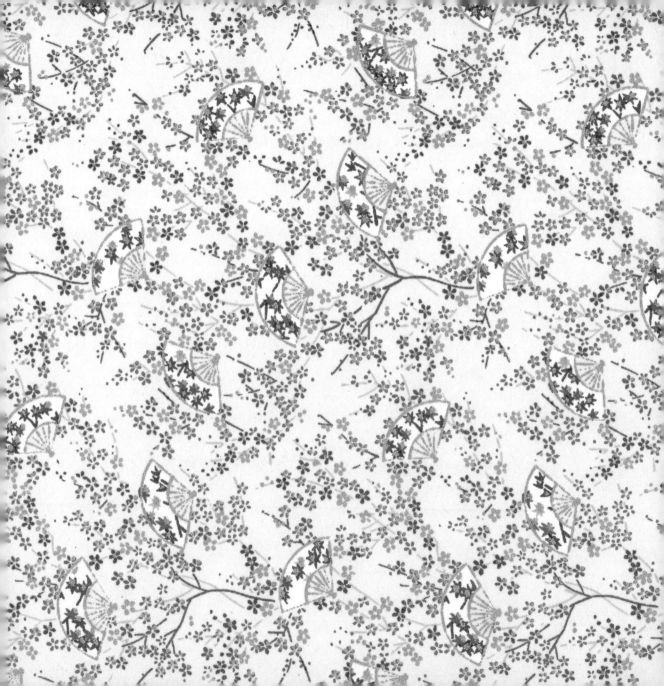

SAILBOAT

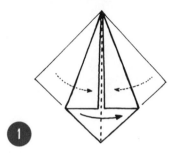

1

2

Outside reverse fold.

3

4

5

Sink point.

6

SMALL BOX

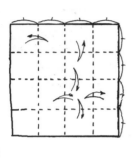

1

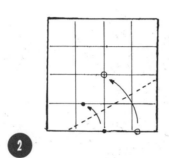

2

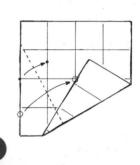

3

4

5

TWELVE-WINGED SPINNING TOP

Start with the colored side of the paper up and fold the area into 16 equal-sized squares, in the order shown.

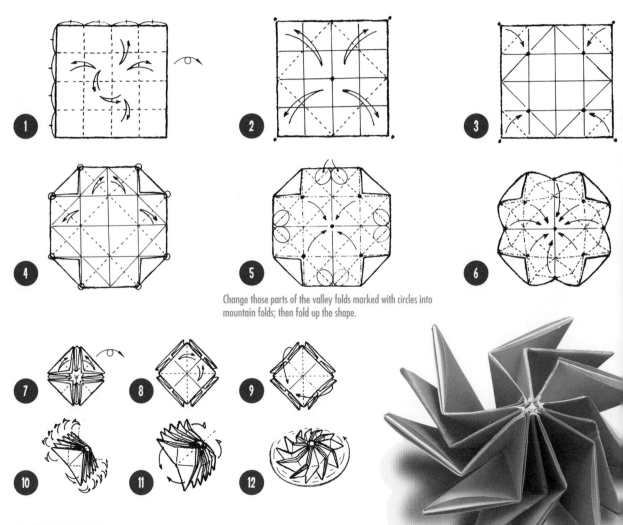

Change those parts of the valley folds marked with circles into mountain folds; then fold up the shape.

SHOOTING STAR

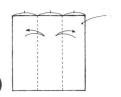

1 Start by placing the paper face up, with your chosen color for the finished Star showing; fold into three equal parts.

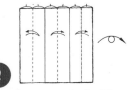

2 Halve all three areas with valley folds and unfold.

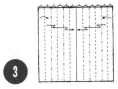

3 Divide each area further with valley folds and make mountain folds where shown, working towards the center.

4

5

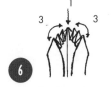

6 You should end up with seven points.

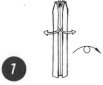

7 Unfold and turn over.

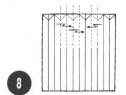

8 Fold only the marked mountain and valley folds.

9 Fold in the order indicated.

10

11 Fold down only the front two layers of corners. On the central line, fold outwards and to the back.

12 Make sharp creases.

13 Finish off the Star.

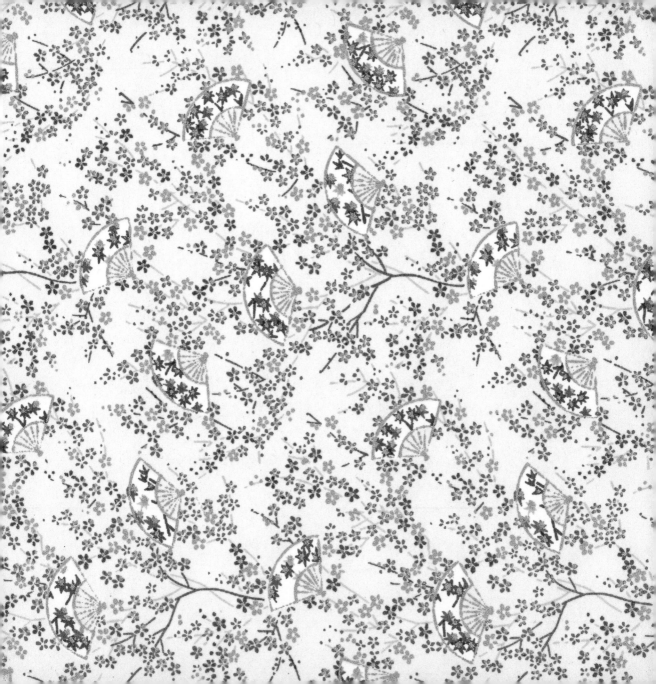